Office XP
FOR
DUMMIES®
QUICK REFERENCE

by Doug Lowe

WILEY

Wiley Publishing, Inc.

Office XP For Dummies® Quick Reference

Published by
Wiley Publishing, Inc.
909 Third Avenue
New York, NY 10022
www.wiley.com

Copyright © 2001 Wiley Publishing, Inc., Indianapolis, Indiana

Published simultaneously in Canada

For general information on our other products and services or to obtain technical support, please contact our Customer Care Department within the U.S. at 800-762-2974, outside the U.S. at 317-572-3993, or fax 317-572-4002.

Wiley also publishes its books in a variety of electronic formats. Some content that appears in print may not be available in electronic books.

Library of Congress Cataloging-in-Publication Data:

Library of Congress Control Number: 2001086268

ISBN: 0-7645-0820-2

Manufactured in the United States of America

10 9 8 7 6 5 4

1O/RX/QU/QT/IN

About the Author

Doug Lowe has written more than 50 computer books, including IDG Books Worldwide's *PowerPoint 2002 For Windows For Dummies, Networking For Dummies (Fifth Edition),* and *Internet Explorer 5.5 For Dummies,* and he knows how to present boring technostuff in a style that is both entertaining and enlightening. He lives in sunny Fresno, California with his wife Debbie, three adorable daughters, and two female golden retrievers. He considers himself significantly outnumbered.

Dedication

To Debbie, Rebecca, Sarah, and Bethany

Acknowledgments

Thanks to all the creative and talented people at Hungry Minds, Inc., especially Mica Johnson, who kept this book on track and made many improvements throughout, Rebekah Mancilla and Kerwin McKenzie who made valuable editorial and technical contributions to ensure that this book would be both readable and accurate, and Steve Hayes who provided vision and support.

Thanks also to the long list of people who worked on previous editions: Kelly Oliver, Michael Lerch, Mary Goodwin, William A. Barton, Jim McCarter, Pam Mourouzis, Michael Simsic, and Jim McCarter.

Publisher's Acknowledgments

We're proud of this book; please register your comments through our online registration form located at www.dummies.com/register.

Some of the people who helped bring this book to market include the following:

Acquisitions, Editorial, and Media Development

Project Editor: Mica Johnson

Senior Acquisitions Editor: Steven Hayes

Copy Editors: Rebekah Mancilla, Beth Parlon

Technical Editor: Kerwin McKenzie

Editorial Manager: Leah Cameron

Media Development Manager: Laura Carpenter

Media Development Supervisor: Richard Graves

Production

Project Coordinator: Nancee Reeves

Layout and Graphics: Brian Drumm, Jacque Schneider, Brian Torwelle, Julie Trippetti, Jeremey Unger

Proofreaders: Nancy Price, TECHBOOKS Production Services

Indexer: TECHBOOKS Production Services

Publishing and Editorial for Technology Dummies
   Richard Swadley, Vice President and Executive Group Publisher
   Andy Cummings, Vice President and Publisher
   Mary C. Corder, Editorial Director

Publishing for Technology Dummies
   Diane Graves Steele, Vice President and Publisher
   Joyce Pepple, Acquisitions Director

Composition Services
   Gerry Fahey, Vice President of Production Services
   Debbie Stailey, Director of Composition Services

Table of Contents

Office XP

You certainly get your money's worth with Office XP. In one convenient bundle, you get a world-class word processor (Word 2002), a spreadsheet program (Excel 2002), a presentation program (PowerPoint 2002), an e-mail program (Outlook 2002), and a database program (Access 2002). Plus, you get a grab-bag of other useful programs. What a bargain!

In this part . . .

- What You See
- Toolbar Table
- The Basics
- What You Can Do

What You See: Office XP Programs

The figure on these two pages shows the four main programs that come with the Standard Edition of Office XP: Word 2002, Excel 2002, PowerPoint 2002, and Outlook 2002. For more information on what you can do with the features that this figure points out, check out the individual sections for each program later in this book.

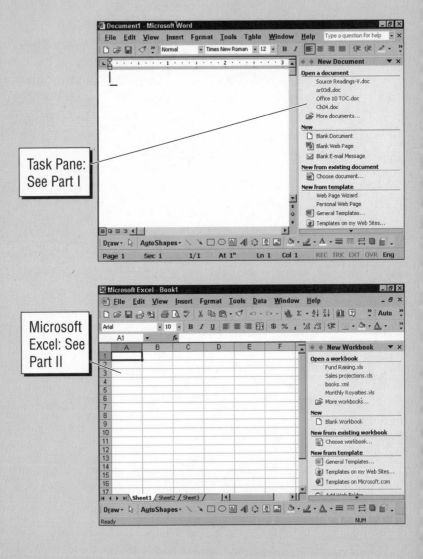

Task Pane:
See Part I

Microsoft
Excel: See
Part II

Microsoft PowerPoint: See Part IV

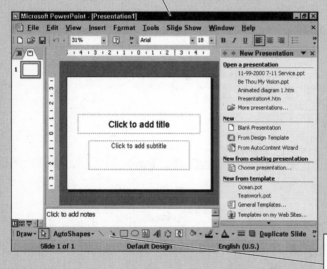

Drawing Toolbar: See Part IV

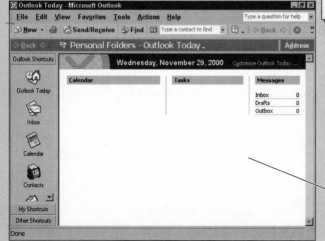

Microsoft Outlook: See Part VI

What You See: Dialog Boxes

In Office programs, you use dialog boxes to enter information like document
or file names, to specify formatting information for text or drawing objects, to
select options for various Office tasks, and so on. If you've used Windows programs before, you're already familiar with most of the elements in Office
dialog boxes — tabs that logically divide the categories of information that
you can access from the dialog box, and controls, such as radio buttons,
check boxes, and text boxes. The figure shows a typical dialog box.

 TIP ▶ If the name of a dialog box control has an underlined letter, such as
Properties, press Alt plus the underlined letter to jump to that field.
This underlining shortcut feature also works for menu command
choices. For example, you can call up the File menu by pressing Alt+F.

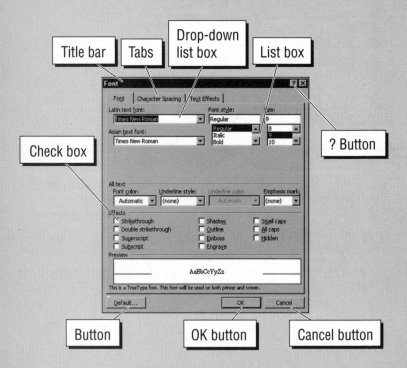

- **? Button:** Lets you access help for a dialog box control. When you click the ? button, the mouse pointer turns into an arrow with a big question mark riding piggy-back. You can then click any control on the dialog box to display helpful information about the control.

- **Button:** A button that ends with ellipses, such as Default..., calls up another dialog box. When you finish with the dialog box that appears, you are returned to the dialog box that you started from.

- **Cancel button:** Closes the dialog box without applying any of the settings or changes that you made.

- **Check box:** Controls an option. Click the check box to add or remove the check.

- **Drop-down list box:** A list box that shows the current selection in the box, followed by a down arrow. Click the down arrow to reveal the choices for the box, then click an option.

- **List box:** A box that contains one or more choices. Click a choice. The box may contain a scroll bar that enables you to view additional choices.

- **OK button:** Accepts the settings or changes that you make on the dialog box.

- **Radio button (not shown):** Also known as an Option button. Radio buttons appear in groups; only one of the buttons in the group can be selected. Click a radio button to select it.

- **Spinner (not shown):** A control that has a numeric value and two arrows, one pointing up and one pointing down. You can increase the number by clicking the up arrow or decrease the number by clicking the down arrow.

- **Tab:** Dialog boxes that contain many controls are often divided into several pages, each with its own tab across the top of the dialog box. Click on one of the tabs to bring up the controls for that tab.

- **Title bar:** The very top of the dialog box contains the dialog box title. You can move the dialog box around the screen by dragging the Title bar.

> **TIP** Note that throughout Office, menus initially show just the commands that you use most often. You can reveal less-often used commands by clicking the double-down arrow that appears at the bottom of a menu, or by simply waiting. If you open a menu but then don't do anything for a few moments, Office automatically displays the less-frequently used commands.

Toolbar Table

All Office programs have one or more toolbars that are loaded with buttons and other controls, which you can click to quickly invoke common functions — such as opening or closing a file, applying common formatting like bold or italics, and so on. The Standard and Formatting toolbars contain buttons and controls that are nearly the same in Word, Excel, and PowerPoint. And many of these buttons also show up from time to time in Access and Outlook.

The following table shows the most commonly used Standard Toolbar buttons:

Tool/Button	Tool name	What You Can Do	Shortcut	See
	New	Creates a new document or file	Ctrl+N	The Big Picture
	Open	Opens an existing document or file	Ctrl+O	The Big Picture
	Save	Saves the current document or file	Ctrl+S	The Big Picture
	E-Mail	Sends a document to an e-mail address	none	Part I
	Search	Searches for information	none	Part I
	Print	Prints a document	Ctrl+P	The Big Picture
	Print Preview	Shows how a document will appear when printed	Ctrl+F2	The Big Picture
	Spelling	Checks the spelling in your document	F7	Part I
	Cut	Cuts selected text and stores it in the clipboard	Ctrl+X	The Basics
	Copy	Copies selected text to the clipboard	Ctrl+C	The Basics
	Paste	Pastes the contents of the clipboard into a document	Ctrl+V	The Basics
	Undo	Undoes the last command or editing operation	Ctrl+Z	The Basics

The following table shows the most-commonly used Formatting Toolbar buttons:

Tool/Button	Tool name	What You Can Do	Shortcut	See
Times New Roman ▾	Font	Choose a font	Ctrl+Shift+F	Parts II, III, and IV
9 ▾	Font Size	Choose a font size	Ctrl+Shift+P	Parts II, III, and IV
B	Bold	Format bold text	Ctrl+B	Parts II, III, and IV
I	Italic	Format italic text	Ctrl+I	Parts II, III, and IV
U	Underline	Format underlined text	Ctrl+U	Parts II, III, and IV
≣	Left	Left-align text	Ctrl+L	Parts II, III, and IV
≣	Center	Center text	Ctrl+E	Parts II, III, and IV
≣	Right	Right-align text	Ctrl+R	Parts II, III, and IV
≣	Justify	Justify text	Ctrl+J	Parts II, III, and IV
≣	Numbering	Creates numbered lists	none	Parts II and IV
≣	Bullets	Creates bulleted lists	none	Parts II and IV
⇐	Decrease indent	Decreases paragraph indentation	none	Parts II, III, and IV
⇒	Increase indent	Increases paragraph indentation	none	Parts II, III, and IV

TIP Most Office toolbars have more controls that fit on the screen at one time. You can click the down arrow that appears at the bottom of each toolbar to see the toolbar controls that didn't fit. Whenever you select a toolbar control in this manner, Office moves the button that you used to the main toolbar so you don't have to go hunting for that button next time.

To move a toolbar around the screen, drag the toolbar by the vertical gray bar that appears on the left edge of the toolbar. You can drag a toolbar to the top, left, bottom, or right edge of the screen, or you can place the toolbar in the middle of the screen as a floater.

 Right-click any toolbar or choose the View⇨Toolbars command to reveal a list of all the toolbars that are available.

The Basics: Starting an Office Program

To start any of the Office XP programs, click the Start button, usually located at the bottom left corner of your screen. Next, point to Programs, and then click the Office program that you want to start. The figure shows the Windows 98 Start menu in action.

 TIP If you can't find the Start button, try moving the mouse all the way to the bottom edge of the screen to see whether the Start button appears. If that doesn't work, point to the top, left, and right edges of the screen until the Start button appears. If all else fails, press Ctrl+Esc to bring up the Start menu.

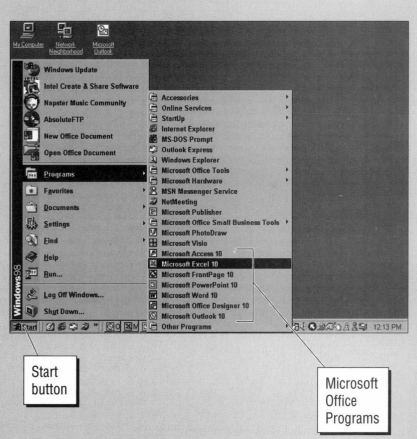

Start button

Microsoft Office Programs

TIP

You can place a shortcut icon to the program that you use most frequently either on the top level of the Start menu or on your desktop. To do this quickly and easily, click Start, point to Programs, and locate the program that you want to make a shortcut for. Then, click and hold the left mouse button on the program and drag the program to where you want it. (If you want the program on the top of the Start menu, drag it to the area of the Start menu over Programs; if you want it on the desktop, drag it there.) Then, whenever you want to open that program, simply click the shortcut icon.

The Basics: Navigating Around an Office Program

Office XP has tried to make the basic layout of the various Office programs as consistent as possible. Here are some tips that will help you find your way around any Office program:

- Each program offers several *views*. For example, Word has Normal view, Web Layout view, Print Layout view, and Outline view. You can change views using the View menu. Word and PowerPoint also display View buttons in the lower-left corner of the screen.

- A Task Pane often appears at the right side of the screen. The Task Pane is used for common functions, such as opening files, searching for information, and formatting documents.

The main portion of the screen contains the document that you're working on. If the entire document does not simultaneously fit on the screen, scroll bars appear at the right and at the bottom of the document area. You can use the scroll bars in three ways:

- Click one of the arrows at either end of the scroll bar to move the document in the direction of the arrow. You can hold down the mouse button to continue scrolling the document.

- Click and drag the box in the scroll bar to move to a specific location in the document. Release the mouse button when you arrive at the part of the document that you want to see.

- Click above or below the box in the scroll bar to move the document one page at a time.

Menu bar

Tool bar

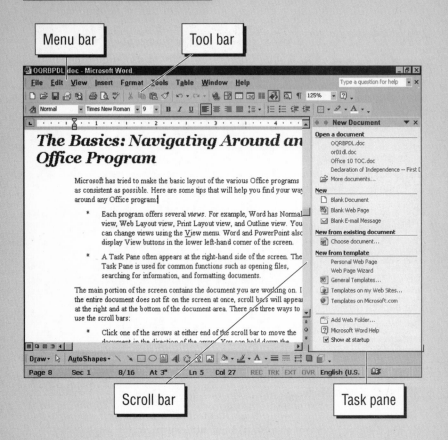

Scroll bar

Task pane

The Basics: Getting Help

Office XP offers many forms of assistance, including extensive helpful information that you can access using the Help command, a friendly animated helper called the Office Assistant, and online help via the Internet.

To call up Help information in an Office program, choose the Help⇨Help command (or, press F1). A Help window similar to the one shown in the figure appears.

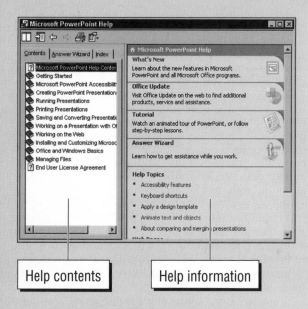

Help contents   Help information

The Help window has three tabs:

- ✔ **Contents:** Displays a table of contents for the entire Help system. Click a topic in the Contents list to reveal more detailed information on that topic. The actual Help information appears in the right side of the Help window.

- ✔ **Answer Wizard:** Lets you type plain English questions rather than searching through the contents. For example, type **How do I add a border?** to learn about borders.

- ✔ **Index:** Displays a detailed index that enables you to search for help on a specific topic.

Office also has an animated help feature called The Office Assistant, which appears on your screen in the form of a character that periodically does cartwheels or dozes off to sleep. You can ask the assistant a question by clicking on him or her, then typing your question. The figure shows an Assistant in action.

 TIP If you don't like the paper-clip Assistant (whose name is "Clippit"), you can choose from six other Assistants that come with Office. Right-click the Assistant and pick the Choose Assistant command from the menu that appears. Then choose the Assistant you want to use. If you don't want to use the Assistant at all, click the Assistant's Options button, then uncheck the Use Office Assistant checkbox in the Options tab.

 TIP A quick way to get help in any Office XP program is to type a question in the Ask a Question box, which appears near the top right corner of any Office XP application window. When you type a question and press the Enter key, a list of possible Help topics appears in a menu below the Ask a Question box. You can then click on one of these Help topics to see more information.

The Basics: Opening a File

You can open a document in Word, Excel, or PowerPoint in any of the following ways:

- ✔ Choose File⇨Open
- ✔ Press Ctrl+O
- ✔ Click the Open button (shown in the margin)

Whichever method you choose, an Open dialog box (similar to the one shown in the figure) appears. (The dialog box shown here is from Word, but the Open dialog box for Excel and PowerPoint are nearly identical.) You can use the controls on this dialog box to navigate through the folders on your hard drive. When you find the file that you want to open, click it once to select it, then click Open. (Or, just double-click the file to open it.)

List most frequently used documents

Select a different folder or drive

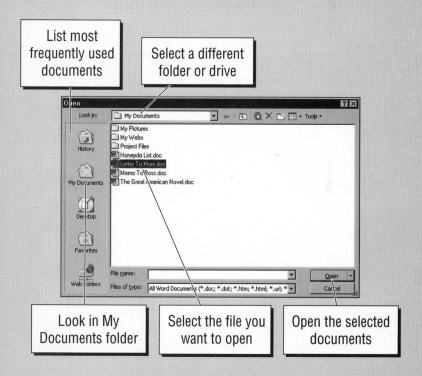

Look in My Documents folder

Select the file you want to open

Open the selected documents

The Basics: Saving a Document

When you save your document, a copy of the document is written to your computer's hard drive so that you can retrieve it later. Here are the three basic ways to save a document:

- ✔ Choose File⇨Save
- ✔ Press Ctrl+S
- ✔ Click the Save button.

The first time you save a new file, Office displays the Save As dialog box as shown in the figure. (This figure shows the Save As dialog box from Excel, but other Office programs use the same format.) You use the Save As dialog box to indicate the drive and folder that you want to save your document in, as well as the name that you want to use for the document. When you're ready to save your document, click the Save button.

Open the My Documents folder

Select a different folder or drive

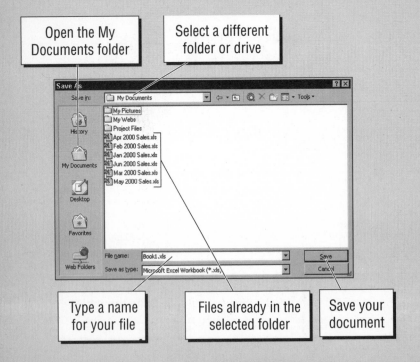

Type a name for your file

Files already in the selected folder

Save your document

TIP You can create a copy of an existing document by opening the document, and then choosing the File⇨Save As command to call up the Save As dialog box. Type a name for the copy, then click Save to create the copy.

The Basics: Printing a Document

To print a document, Choose the File⇨Print command. This action calls up the Print dialog box, shown in the figure. (The figure shows the Word version of the Print dialog box. Other Office programs have minor variations.)

Choose the
printer

Indicate how
many copies to
print

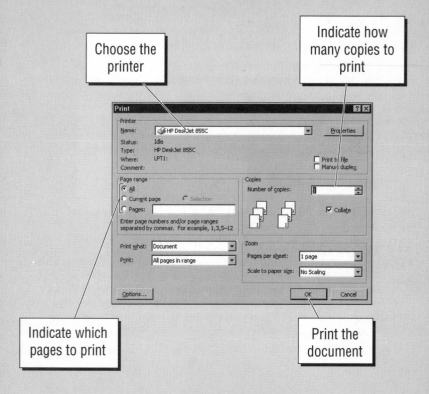

Indicate which
pages to print

Print the
document

 To print a single copy of your document quickly — without fussing with the Print dialog box — click the Print button in the Standard toolbar.

 Use the Print Preview button to see how a document will appear when printed before you send the document to the printer.

The Basics: Exiting an Office Program

After you're finished working in an Office program, you should exit the program using one of the following methods:

- ✔ Choose the File⇨Exit command

- ✔ Press Alt+F4

- ✔ Click the Close button located in the top right corner of the program window. The Close button is marked by an X, proving the old adage that X does, indeed, mark the spot.

You cannot exit a program until you have saved your work. If you try to exit without saving your work, Office displays a dialog box similar to the one shown in the figure.

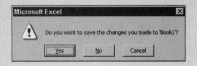

Microsoft Excel

Do you want to save the changes you made to 'Book1'?

Yes   No   Cancel

WARNING Never just turn off your computer while a program is running. This can damage your computer and leave hacked-up file parts strewn about your hard drive. Always exit all programs that are running *before* you turn off your computer, and notify Windows that you are about to turn off your computer by clicking the Start button and choosing the Shut Down command.

What You Can Do

Computerize Your Mailing List

One of the most powerful features of Word 2002 is its Mail Merge feature, which enables you to create personalized letters from a list of names and addresses. You can create the list of names and addresses directly in Word, or you can create the address list in Access or Outlook. In addition to letters, you can also print envelopes, labels, and directories.

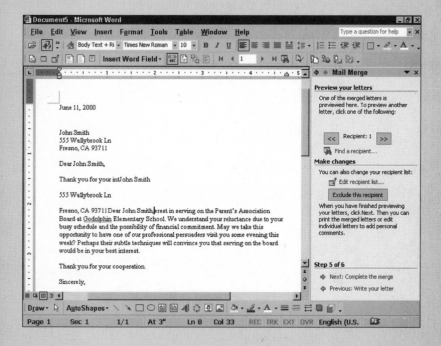

1. Get started by

Creating a Word Address List for your mailing addresses, Part II

Creating a letter for your mailing, Part II

2. Work on your project by

Merging the letters, Part II

Printing labels and envelopes, Part II

E-mailing merged letters, Part II

3. Add finishing touches by

Printing a directory of your mailing list, Part II

Creating an Access database for your mailing addresses, Part V

Creating an Access query for more selective mailings, Part V

What You Can Do

Collaborating on a Document

One of the greatest strengths of the suite of Office products is that they allow you to work together with other users on documents. You can collaborate on documents that you create with Word, Excel, PowerPoint, or Access, but Word and Excel have the strongest features for online collaboration. The figure shows a Word document with comments and edits made by several users. (Now you know why Benjamin Franklin turned down the offer to write the Declaration of Independence.)

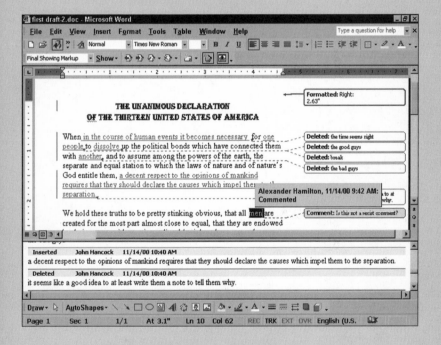

1. Get started by

Creating an e-mail contact for each person who is to work on the project, Part VI

Creating a distribution list of all contacts for the project, Part VI

Creating the first draft of your document in Word, Part II

2. Work on your project by

Enabling the track changes feature for the document, Part II

Sending the document to the project's distribution list, Part I

(Team members) Reviewing and editing the document and returning it to the sender, Part II

3. Add finishing touches by

Accepting or rejecting changes made by the project team members, Part II

Sending the revised document for additional reviews, Part I

Scheduling online meetings, Part VI

What You Can Do

Create a Web Site

Some editions of Office XP include FrontPage, a sophisticated Web-site development program. You don't have to have FrontPage, however, to create a Web site: All Office programs have the ability to save documents as Web pages, so you can use Word, Excel, or PowerPoint to create a basic Web site. The figure shows a simple Web page that I created with Word.

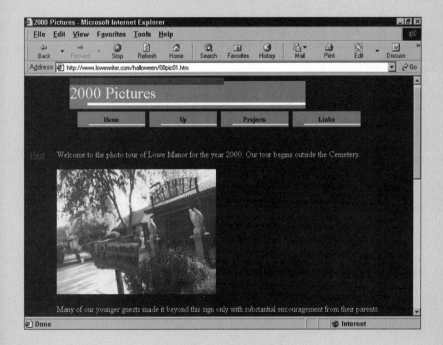

1. Get started by

Adding a Web folder for your Web site, Part I

Scanning pictures that you want to include on your Web page, Part VII

Creating a Web page in Word using the Web Page Wizard, Part II

2. Work on your project by

Editing the page in Web Layout view, Part II

Inserting pictures that you scanned, Part VII

Adding hyperlinks, Part II

3. Add finishing touches by

Creating additional pages, Part II

Using a theme, Part II

Adding Link bars, Part II

Doing Common Chores

In this part, you find out how to work with tasks that are fairly common among the different Office programs. Some of these tasks are reasonably basic; others are more advanced. You can be sure, however, that these tasks work mostly the same way in the different programs of the Office XP suite.

In this part . . .

Clipboard

The *Clipboard* is the Windows feature that enables you to move data within a file, between files, or between programs. Microsoft Office XP improves on the basic Clipboard feature found in all Windows programs by allowing you to hold more than one item in the Clipboard. The following sections describe how to copy and move data using the Clipboard.

Copying or cutting data

You can make a copy of a selection of a document and paste that copy somewhere else. The procedure for copying data is the same whether the new location for the copied data is in the same document, in a different document using the same program (such as copying from a Word document to a Word document), or in a different program (such as copying from Word to Excel).

Cutting is similar to copying, except that when you cut a selection, the information that you cut is deleted from the document. A copy of the cut information is added to the clipboard so you can paste a copy of it elsewhere in the document (or in another document). In effect, copying enables you to make a duplicate copy of information, whereas cutting enables you to move information from one location to another.

To copy or cut text, follow these steps:

1. Select (or highlight) the information that you want to copy or cut.

The easiest way to select text is to position your cursor at the beginning of the selection and press the left mouse button. Continue to hold down the mouse button and drag the mouse so that you highlight all the text that you want to select. Release the mouse button and the text is selected. This procedure can also be used to select entire cells in Excel.

2. To copy the selection, choose Edit⇨Copy, press Ctrl+C, or click the Copy button on the Standard toolbar.

The Cut button on the Standard toolbar.

The Standard toolbar is the toolbar that appears by default along the top of your application window. If you don't see a toolbar that you want to use, click View⇨Toolbars. This shows you a list of all the available toolbars for that application.

3. Move the cursor to the location where you want to insert the text.

4. Choose Edit⇨Paste, press Ctrl+V, or click the Paste button on the Standard toolbar.

When you paste text, the Paste Options button (shown in the margin) appears near the inserted text. You can click this button to reveal a menu of options that gives you a choice among retaining the text's original formatting, formatting the text using the formatting of the destination, or inserting the text without any formatting information. (Additional options may appear on this menu, depending on the type of data that you are pasting and the program that you are working with.)

Dragging and dropping text

You can move text from one location to another by using the drag-and-drop technique. This action works only when you're moving text or pictures within the same document.

Before using this feature, you must make sure that the drag-and-drop option is enabled. To do this, select Tools⇨Options. When the Options dialog box appears, click the Edit tab and make sure that the drag-and-drop feature is checked. (In Word and PowerPoint, this option is called Drag-and-Drop Text Editing, but in Excel it's called Allow Cell Drag and Drop.)

When the drag-and-drop feature is enabled, you can use it as follows:

1. Select the text that you want to move.

2. Place the mouse pointer anywhere over the selected text and then press and hold the left mouse button.

3. Drag the text to the location where you want to move the text. (A little box will appear beneath the mouse pointer as you move the text to remind you that you are dragging text around.)

4. Release the mouse button.

To copy rather than move text, press and hold the Ctrl key while dragging the text. (A + sign will appear below the mouse pointer while you move the mouse to remind you that you are dragging text.)

The Office Clipboard

The Office Clipboard feature lets you gather up to 24 items of text or graphics from any Office program, then selectively paste them into an Office document. The Office Clipboard appears in the task pane at the right side of the screen, where it lists all of the items you have copied or cut to the Office Clipboard. This figure shows the Office Clipboard in action.

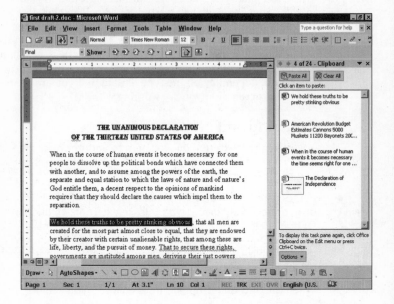

To paste an item from the Office Clipboard, first click to mark the location in the document where you want to insert the item, and then click the item in the Office Clipboard that you want to insert.

Items that you cut or copy are added to the Office Clipboard only if the Office Clipboard is active. You can activate the Office Clipboard in several ways:

✔ Choose Edit⇨Office Clipboard

✔ Press Ctrl+C twice

✔ Copy or cut two items consecutively, without doing anything else in between

The Office Clipboard icon appears in the taskbar whenever the Office Clipboard is active. As long as this icon appears, items that you cut or copy are added to the Office Clipboard, even if the Office Clipboard is not visible in the taskbar of the program you are working in.

To remove an item from the Office Clipboard, right-click the item and choose Delete from the menu that appears.

E-Mail

If your computer is connected to a network or to the Internet, you can send a copy of the document that you're working on to a friend or co-worker via e-mail by using the File⇨Send To command. Some variations of the File⇨Send To command are the following:

- ✔ **Mail Recipient:** Sends a copy of the document as an e-mail message. The text of your document is inserted directly into the body of the message.

- ✔ **Mail Recipient (As Attachment):** Sends a copy of the document as an attachment of the e-mail.

- ✔ **Mail Recipient (For Review):** Attaches a copy of the document file to the e-mail message and inserts the message "Please review the attached document" in the body of the message.

- ✔ **Routing Recipient:** Allows you to send the document to a list of users. The users in the list receive the document one at a time. When each user is finished reviewing the document, he or she can forward the document to the next user in the route list by choosing the File⇨Send To⇨Next Routing Recipient command.

To e-mail a document as an attachment to an e-mail message, follow these steps:

1. Choose File⇨Send To⇨Mail Recipient (as Attachment). This summons the New Message dialog box, as shown in the figure. (The figure shows how the New Message dialog box appears if you use Outlook as your e-mail program. If you use a different e-mail program, your New Message dialog box may have a different appearance.)

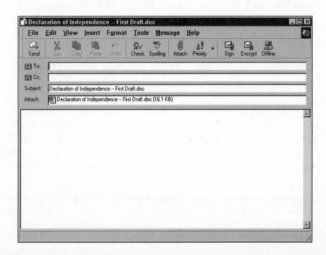

If the program asks you to specify a user profile, select the profile that you normally use in sending and receiving e-mail. User profiles control things like which e-mail services you have access to and where your address book is stored. If more than one person uses your computer, you can set up a separate profile for each user. If possible, talk to the person responsible for setting up your e-mail system about configuring your user profile for you.

2. Type the e-mail address of the person that you want to send the document to in the To text box.

 If you have the recipient's e-mail address on file in your Address book, click the To button to summon the Address book. Then, select the correct recipient and click OK to return to the New Message dialog box.

3. Type a subject for your message in the Subject text box.

4. Type a message on the message body area of the New Message dialog box.

 5. Click the Send button (shown in the margin) to send the message.

Searching

Office XP comes with a powerful search feature that lets you find missing files. You can search for files in folders on your computer's hard drive, in your Outlook folders, and in your Web folders. The Search feature utilizes the Office XP Task Pane, which appears in a separate pane on the right side of the screen.

 Don't confuse the Search feature with the Find command, which locates text within the document that you are working on. For information about using the Find command in Word or Excel, see Parts II and III.

To search for a file in any Office program, follow these steps:

 1. Click the Search button (shown in the margin). Or choose File⇨Search. This summons the Search Pane, as depicted in the figure.

2. Type the text that you want to search for in the Search Text field.

3. Click the Search button.

4. Sing your favorite show tunes while Office searches for documents that contain the text that you typed. (If others are nearby, just hum.)

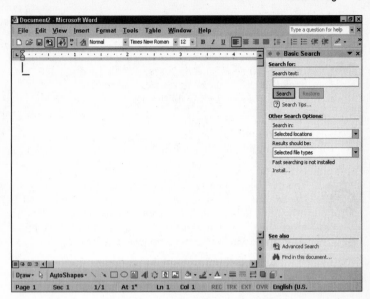

If you get bored, you can cancel the search by clicking the Stop button.

5. Smile appreciatively when Office displays the results of your search, as shown in the figure.

6. To open one of the documents listed in the search results, click the document name.

When you point to one of the documents listed in the search results, a down arrow appears next to the document name. You can click this down arrow to reveal a menu of actions that you can choose from, including editing the document, creating a new file based on the document, and displaying the document properties.

7. After you are finished, click the Close button to hide the Search Pane. (The Close button is the X located in the top-right corner of the Search Pane.)

You can click the Advanced Search button, located at the bottom of the Search Pane, to search for files based on advanced criteria. The Advanced Search options allow you to search for files based on more than 50 document properties, such as the file name, creation date, size, owner, number of pages, and so on.

Speech

One of the major new features of Office XP is speech recognition, which enables you to dictate text into your documents and issue menu commands by speaking rather than by typing or clicking the mouse. Although it is not perfect, speech recognition can take dictation with 90 percent or better accuracy if you use the right hardware and if you configure speech recognition properly.

For speech recognition to work well, you need to have a beefy computer. Microsoft recommends at least a 400MHz Pentium II computer with 128MB or more of RAM for satisfactory speech performance. If you have a slower computer or less than 128MB of RAM, the speech feature works so slowly that you won't want to use it.

You should also invest in a headset microphone. Handheld microphones or boom microphones attached to your monitor don't provide sound that is consistent enough for speech recognition to reliably figure out what you're saying.

Speech recognition works in all Office XP programs, but is not installed by default when you install Office XP on your computer. If speech recognition is not installed on your computer, you can install it by firing up Word and choosing the Tools⇔Speech command. Word notices that Speech recognition isn't installed and automatically installs it.

For speech recognition to work best, you should train it to recognize your voice. To train speech recognition, you just read aloud text that appears on the screen. Speech recognition listens to your speech, matches it up with what it's expecting you to say, and records the subtle nuances of your voice. The training session takes about 15 minutes.

You can train the speech recognition feature when you install it, or you can train it later by choosing Tools on the Language toolbar (described the next section), then choosing Training.

The Language toolbar

After you have trained speech recognition, you see the Language toolbar displayed near the top of your screen, as shown in the figure.

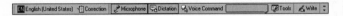

The functions of the Language toolbar buttons that you use for speech recognition are as follows:

✔ **Microphone:** Click once to turn on the microphone for speech recognition. Click again to turn the microphone off.

✔ **Dictation:** Click to enter dictation mode.

✔ **Voice command:** Click to enter voice command mode.

Dictation

To dictate text into an Office document, follow these steps:

1. Position the insertion point where you want to insert the text that you dictate.

2. Click the Microphone button in the Language toolbar to turn on the microphone. (Skip this step if you have already turned the microphone on.)

3. Click the Dictation button in the Language toolbar to activate dictation mode.

4. Speak the words that you want dictated clearly, in a normal tone of voice. The words won't appear on the screen at first. Instead, a series of shaded periods appears while speech recognition figures out what you said. In a moment, the shaded periods are replaced by the words you spoke, or (hopefully) something close.

Pause once in awhile to let Speech recognition catch up.

5. When you are finished dictating, click the Microphone button to turn off the microphone.

6. Correct any dictation mistakes by right-clicking any incorrect words and then choosing the correct word from the list of alternatives that appears. Or, simply delete the incorrect text and retype the correct text in its place.

Don't forget to turn off the microphone by clicking the Microphone button when you are finished dictating. If you leave the microphone on, any stray noises that the microphone picks up — such as a sneeze — finds its way into your document. And who knows how speech recognition will translate your sneezes.

To dictate punctuation, just say the name of the punctuation mark that you want to use, such as "Period," "Comma," or "Semicolon." For quotation marks, say "Open quote" or "Close quote."

Voice commands

To speak commands to an Office program, click the Microphone button to turn on the microphone if you have not already done so, then click the Voice Commands button. Now you can tell the computer what you want it to do.

To use menu commands, just say the name of the menu option. For example, to activate the File menu, say "File." Then, to select the Open command, say "Open."

When you are in a dialog box, you can speak the name of a button or other dialog box control to activate the button or control. For example, saying "OK" clicks the OK button. In the Font dialog box, saying "Strikethrough" checks the Strikethrough option.

Here are some additional words you can say to move around in a document or dialog box:

Enter	Cancel (same as Escape)	Down
Backspace		Left
Delete	Right-click	Right
Space	End	Page Up
Spacebar	Home	Page Down
Escape	Up	

Spell Checking

Office XP is designed so that you can check your spelling in any of its applications. You can check your spelling in two ways, depending on which program you're using. First, if you are using either Word or PowerPoint, the program can check your spelling as you type — marking misspelled words so that you can immediately correct them. Second, all the Office XP programs can check your spelling after you have typed your document, so you can forget about spelling as you write, with the knowledge that you can correct any mistakes later on.

Spell checking as you type

Unless you disable the Office spell checker, both Word 2002 and PowerPoint 2002 check the spelling of your words as you type. The program underlines any misspelled words with a wavy red line.

To correct a misspelled word, right-click the word. Then pick the correct spelling from the pull-down menu that appears.

If the correct spelling does not appear in the list when you right-click the misspelled word, press the Esc key and manually correct the spelling.

If the automatic spell checker incorrectly flags a word as misspelled, you can add the word to the Spelling dictionary so that the word won't be flagged in the future. To do so, right-click the word, then choose Add to Dictionary from the pull-down menu.

You can also tell Word or PowerPoint to ignore an incorrect spelling by right-clicking the misspelled word and choosing Ignore All.

If you don't like the automatic spell checker, you can disable the feature in either Word or PowerPoint by following these steps:

1. Choose Tools⇨Options to open the Options dialog box.

2. In Word, click the Spelling and Grammar tab. In PowerPoint, click the Spelling and Style tab.

3. Click the Check Spelling as You Type check box to deselect this option.

4. Click the OK button.

If you want to turn the automatic spell checker back on, just repeat the procedure, clicking the Check Spelling as You Type option to select it.

Spell checking after you type

If you disable the as-you-type spell checker in Word and PowerPoint, you can always spell check your work after the fact. And you can spell check this way in all the Office XP programs. Here's how:

1. Choose Tools⇨Spelling (in Word, the command is Tools⇨Spelling and Grammar), press F7, or click the Spelling button in the Standard toolbar (shown in the margin).

Whichever method you choose, the spell checker comes to life and begins checking your document's spelling from the current cursor position. If the spell checker finds a misspelled word, the Spelling dialog box appears.

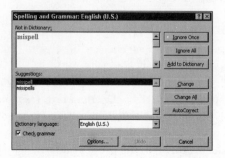

2. Depending on whether the word is misspelled, take one of the following actions:

- If the word really is misspelled, select the correct spelling from the list of suggested spellings that appears in the dialog box and click the Change button.

- If the correct spelling doesn't appear among the suggestions, type the correct spelling in the Not in Dictionary box and click the Change button.

- If the word is correctly spelled, click the Ignore button. Or click the Ignore All button to ignore any subsequent occurrences of the word.

3. Repeat Step 2 until the spell checker gives up. After the spell checker finishes, a message appears to tell you it's done.

Task Pane

The task pane is a new Office XP feature that places commonly used functions in a separate pane on the right side of the screen. You can summon the task pane by choosing the View⇨Task Pane command. The task pane also appears when you call up a feature that uses it, such as Mail Merge in Word or Custom Animations in PowerPoint.

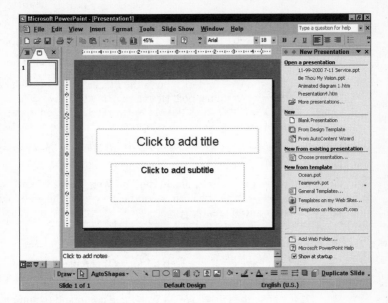

Here are some tips for working with the task pane:

✔ The drop-down list at the top of the task pane lets you choose which pane you want to view in the task pane. The choices available in all Office applications are New, Clipboard, Search, and Insert Clipart. Additional choices appear depending on which Office program you are using.

✔ You can quickly hide the task pane by clicking the close button (the "X" located in the top right corner of the task pane).

✔ You can increase the size of the task pane by dragging the left border of the task pane.

✔ The Forward and Back buttons that appear at the top-left corner of the task pane work much like the Forward and Back buttons in a Web browser, allowing you to recall previous task pane displays.

Web Folders

A *Web folder* is a shortcut to a Web server that you can use to publish Web documents. Web folders make saving documents to a Web server as easy as saving documents to an ordinary folder on your hard drive.

Creating a Web folder

To create a Web folder, follow these steps in any Office application:

1. Choose File⇨Save As to summon the Save As dialog box.

2. Click the Web folders icon in the Places bar on the left edge of the Save As dialog box. (If you're using Windows Millennium or Windows 2000, click the My Network Places icon instead.) A list of existing Web folders appears in the Save As dialog box.

3. Click the Create New Folder button. The Add Web Folder Wizard appears.

4. Follow the instructions in the Add Web Folder Wizard. You are asked to enter the address of the server for the Web folder that you want to create.

Saving a document to a Web folder

After you have created a Web folder, you can use any Office application to save documents to the server by following these steps:

1. Choose the File⇨Save As Web Page command to summon the Save As dialog box.

2. Click the Web Folders icon in the Places bar on the left edge of the Save As dialog box to display a list of your Web folders. (If you're using Windows Millennium Edition or Windows 2000, click the My Network Places icon instead.)

3. Double-click the Web folder that you want to save the document to.

4. If you are asked to enter a user-id and password, do so.

5. Type a name for the document in the File Name field.

6. Click the Save button.

When you save a document using the Save As Web Page command, any supporting files, such as backgrounds, bullets, and images, are saved as well. You can also click the Change Title button on the Save As dialog box to change the title of your Web page.

Word 2002

Microsoft Office XP comes with the latest and greatest version of Microsoft's premier word processing program, Microsoft Word 2002. In this part, I cover the basics of using Word 2002. You can find lots more information in *Word 2002 For Dummies,* by Dan Gookin, published by Hungry Minds, Inc.

In this part . . .

Borders

To add a border around a text paragraph, follow these steps:

1. Place the insertion point anywhere in the paragraph that you want to add a border to.

2. Choose Format⇨Borders and Shading to open the Borders and Shading dialog box.

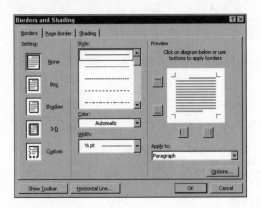

3. Select the type of border that you want from the options in the Setting area of the dialog box's Borders tab (Box, Shadow, 3-D, or Custom, for example). Or click None if you want to remove the border.

4. Select a line style from the Style list, a color from the Color list, and a line width from the Width list if you don't like the default settings.

   Scroll through the entire list of styles; Word offers lots of inter-esting lines from which to choose. If you want each side of the border to have a different style, select the style and then click the appropriate button in the Preview area to apply the style to just that edge. After you change the style, the border around the mock paragraph in the Preview area changes so that you can see how your text appears with the border styles that you selected.

5. Click OK or press Enter.

To get rid of a border, choose Format⇨Borders and Shading and then choose None for the border type.

Note that the Borders and Shading dialog box includes tabs that let you create a border around the entire page or apply shading to text.

Browsing Through a Document

To browse quickly through a document, use the Browse control located at the bottom of the scroll bar, as shown in the margin.

After you click the Select Browse Object button sandwiched between the two double-arrow controls, a menu appears that enables you to access several navigation features from one convenient location, as shown in the following figure:

Two of the buttons on this menu invoke the familiar Edit⇨Go to and Edit⇨Find commands. The ten remaining buttons change the unit by which the document is browsed after you click the double up or double down arrow controls immediately above and below the Select Browse Object button. The following table describes the function of each of the 12 buttons that appear on the Browse menu.

Button	What It Does
→	Invokes the Edit⇨Go to command.
🔍	Invokes the Edit⇨Find command.
✏	Browse by edits (works in conjunction with revision tracking).
☱	Browse by headings, as indicated by standard heading styles.
🖼	Browse by graphic objects.
▦	Browse by Word table object
{a}	Browse by Word fields
🗇	Browse by endnote
🗇	Browse by footnote

cont.

Button	What It Does
	Browse by comments
	Browse by section
	Browse by page

TIP

Another way to browse your document efficiently is to use the Document Map. *See also* "Document Map."

Bulleted Lists

To create a bulleted list, follow this procedure:

1. Type one or more paragraphs that you want to add bullets to.

2. Select the paragraphs that you want to add bullets to by dragging the mouse over them.

3. Click the Bullets button on the Formatting toolbar.

To add more items to the bulleted list, position the cursor at the end of one of the bulleted paragraphs and press Enter. Because the bullet is part of the paragraph format, the bullet format carries over to the new paragraph.

The Bullets button works like a toggle: Click the button once to add bullets and click the button again to remove them. To remove bullets from an entire list, select all the paragraphs in the list and click the Bullets button.

TIP

If you want to create a bulleted list as you compose your text, start by formatting the first paragraph with a bullet. (Either type the text and then format it or create the formatting and then add the text. Word is versatile enough to work both ways.) Word carries the bullet format over to subsequent paragraphs as you type them. After you finish typing your last bulleted paragraph, press Enter and then click the Bullets button again to deactivate bullet formatting.

To change the appearance of the bullet, choose Format⇨Bullets and Numbering and click the Bulleted tab. If the bullet style that you want appears in the Bullets and Numbering dialog box, click that style and then click OK. Otherwise, select any of the bullet styles, then click the Customize button to summon the Customize Bulleted List dialog box. You can then pick whichever oddball bullet character makes you happy.

See also "Formatting Web Pages" for info about formatting bullets for Web pages.

Columns

To create multiple columns in your Word document:

1. Click the Columns button on the Standard toolbar to open the drop-down menu, as shown in the following figure:

2. Drag the mouse to pick the number of columns that you want. For example, if you want two columns in your document, drag the mouse over the columns until you have highlighted two of them. (The figure shows two columns selected.)

3. Release the mouse button.

Voilá! The document appears formatted with the number of columns that you selected.

When you create columns, Word automatically switches you to Print Layout view so you can see how the columns will appear when printed. If you want, you can switch back to Normal view by choosing View⇨Normal. In Normal view, the text is formatted according to the width of the column, but the columns don't appear on-screen side by side.

For a quick glimpse of how the columns appear after you print them, choose File⇨Print Preview. After you have a good look, click the Close button to return to your document.

The Columns button enables you to set the number of columns, but the button doesn't enable you to control the size of each column or the amount of space between columns. To set the size of the columns and the space between them, choose Format⇨Columns and play with its settings.

For more information, check out *Word 2002 For Dummies*.

Document Map

The *Document Map* is a cool feature that enables you to view your document's outline side-by-side with the text, as shown here:

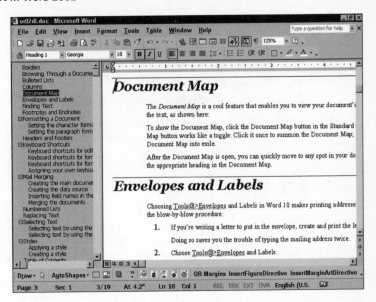

 To show the Document Map, click the Document Map button in the Standard toolbar. The Document Map button works like a toggle: Click it once to summon the Document Map; click it again to send the Document Map into exile. (If you can't find the Document Map button, use the View⇨Document Map command instead.)

After the Document Map is open, you can quickly move to any spot in your document simply by clicking the appropriate heading in the Document Map.

Envelopes and Labels

You can print addresses on envelopes easily in Word by choosing Tools⇨Letters and Mailings⇨Envelopes and Labels. Here's the blow-by-blow procedure:

1. If you're writing a letter to put in the envelope, create and print the letter first.

Doing this saves you the trouble of typing the mailing address twice.

2. Choose Tools⇨Letters and Mailing⇨Envelopes and Labels.

The Envelopes and Labels dialog box appears.

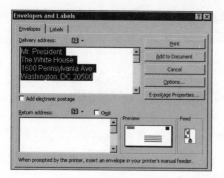

3. Check the address in the Delivery Address field.

Usually, Word can automatically find the mailing address from an ordinary letter. If not, you must enter the address yourself.

If you want a return address printed on the envelope, type the return address in the space provided. (Notice that you can set a default return address by using the Tools⇨Options command, clicking the User Info tab, and typing your return address into the space provided.)

4. Insert an envelope into your printer.

The Feed option in the Envelopes dialog box indicates how you should insert the envelope into the printer. If you want to feed the envelope differently, click the Envelope icon in the Feed area of the Envelopes dialog box to open the Envelope Options dialog box. Select the feeding method that you prefer and then click OK.

5. Click the Print button.

That's all!

If you want to print a label instead of an envelope, click the Labels tab that appears at the top of the Envelopes and Labels dialog box. You can then change the address if necessary, type a return address if you want one, and select whether to print a single label or an entire page of the same label. Then, insert a blank sheet of labels into your printer and click the Print button.

Finding Text

You can choose Edit⇨Find to find text anywhere in a document. Just follow these steps:

1. Choose Edit⇨Find or press Ctrl+F to open the Find and Replace dialog box.

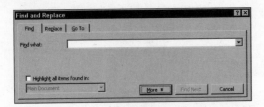

2. In the Find What text box, type the text that you want to find.

   You can type a single word or a phrase. Spaces are allowed.

3. Click the Find Next button.

4. Wait a second while Word searches your document.

   After Word finds the text, the program highlights the text on-screen. The Find dialog box remains on-screen so that you can click the Find Next button to find yet another occurrence of the text. After Word can find no more occurrences of the text, you see the following message in a separate dialog box:

   ```
   Word has finished searching the document.
   ```

5. Click OK and get on with your life.

   You can bail out of the Find and Replace dialog box by clicking the Cancel button or pressing Esc.

You can change how Word searches for your text by clicking the More button in the Find and Replace dialog box to reveal a set of additional search options. The following options are available:

Search Option	What It Does
Search:	Enables you to specify the direction in which Word searches the document for text. The choices are Up, Down, and All. If you choose Up or Down, Word stops at the beginning or end of the document and asks whether you want to continue the search. If you specify All, Word automatically searches the entire document.
Match case	Indicates whether it matters that the text appears in uppercase or lowercase letters.
Find whole words only	Finds your text only if the text appears as a whole word. For example, if you type the word versa, Word ignores any appearance of the word versatile because the targeted letters are not a whole word.
Use wildcards	Enables you to include wildcard characters in the Find What text box. Here are three of the most useful wildcards:

Search Option	What It Does
?	Finds a single occurrence of any character. For example, f?t finds *fat* or *fit*.
*	Finds any combination of characters. For example, **b*t** finds any combination of characters that begins with *b* and ends with *t*, such as *bat, bait, ballast,* or *bacteriologist*.
[abc]	Finds any one of the characters enclosed in the brackets. For example, b[ai]t finds bat or bit but not bet or but.
Sounds like	Finds text that is phonetically similar to the search text, even if the spelling varies.
Find all word forms	Searches for all forms of the search text word. For example, if you search for stink, Word also finds stank and stunk.
Format	Enables you to search for text that has specific formatting applied — for example, to search for text formatted in the Arial font or with red type.
Special	Enables you to search for special characters, such as paragraph or tab marks.
No formatting	Removes any formatting options that you previously specified with the Format button.

Footnotes and Endnotes

Follow these steps to add footnotes or endnotes to your documents:

1. Place the cursor where you want the footnote reference number to appear in your text.

2. Choose Insert⇨Reference⇨Footnote to open the Footnote and Endnote dialog box.

3. If you want the note to appear at the bottom of the page, check the Footnotes option. To create a note that appears at the end of the document, click the Endnotes option.

   Note: The first time you choose Insert⇨Reference⇨Footnote, the Footnotes option is selected. Any time after that, the default setting is whatever you chose the last time you inserted a footnote or endnote. As a result, you only need to worry about selecting Footnotes or Endnotes if you're changing from footnotes to endnotes or back again.

4. Click Insert.

   A separate Footnotes or Endnotes pane opens at the bottom of the screen, where you can type your footnote or endnote.

5. Click the Close button that appears in the Footnotes or Endnotes pane after you finish typing in the footnote or endnote.

   The Footnotes or Endnotes pane disappears.

   Alternatively, you can just click back in the document to continue editing the document while leaving the Footnotes or Endnotes window open.

Word automatically numbers footnotes for you and keeps the numbers in sequence as you insert and delete footnotes. Word also automatically formats footnotes so that a footnote always appears at the bottom of the page in which the footnote is referenced, if possible. Long footnotes may span up to several pages.

For an extra-quick way to create a footnote, press Ctrl+Alt+F.

To recall the Footnotes pane, choose View⇨Footnotes. You can then use the drop-down list that appears in the Footnotes pane to display endnotes instead of footnotes.

If you goof up a footnote, double-click the footnote reference in the text. This opens the Footnote pane and displays the footnote. You can then edit the note however you see fit.

To delete a footnote, select its footnote reference in the text and press Delete.

For more information about footnotes, see *Word 2002 For Dummies*.

Formatting a Document

Word gives you more ways to format your document than any mere mortal could ever need or hope for. The following sections present the more common formatting procedures.

Setting the character format

You can set character formats by using the formatting keyboard shortcuts or the buttons that appear in the Formatting toolbar. **See also** "Keyboard Shortcuts." Or you can use the following procedure to apply character formats via the Format⇨Font command:

1. Highlight the text that you want to apply the formatting to.

   If you skip this step, Word applies formatting to all new text that you type until you call up the Format⇨Font command again.

2. Choose Format⇨Font.

   The Font dialog box appears.

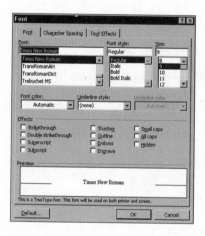

3. Play with the controls in the Font dialog box to set the Font, the Font style (bold, italic, and so on), and the Size. Select any of the Effects area check boxes that you want (Strikethrough, Superscript, and so on), and use the drop-down list boxes to set the Font color, Underline style, and Underline color.

   The Preview box at the bottom of the dialog box shows how text appears after Word applies the formatting options that you selected.

4. Click OK after you have the character format just the way you want it.

You can quickly set character formats by selecting the text to which you want the formats applied and then using one of the buttons on the Formatting toolbar or the keyboard shortcuts listed in the table in the section "Keyboard Shortcuts." Alternatively, you can use the keyboard shortcut or click the button to enable the format, type some text, and then use the shortcut or button again to disable the format.

To quickly remove character formatting, highlight the text that was formatted incorrectly and press Ctrl+space.

Setting the paragraph format

Follow these steps to apply paragraph formats by using the Format⇨Paragraph command:

1. Click anywhere in the paragraph that you want to format.

You don't need to select the entire paragraph as long as the insertion point is somewhere in the paragraph that you want to format.

2. Choose Format⇨Paragraph.

The Paragraph dialog box appears.

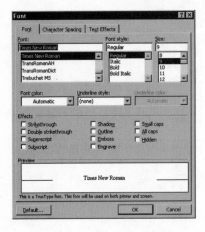

3. Play with the controls to set the paragraph's alignment, indentation, and spacing.

You have lots of controls to play with, and you may not know which one to choose. Fortunately, you can monitor the effect of each setting in the Preview box that appears in the Paragraph dialog box.

4. Click OK after you finish formatting your paragraph.

You can quickly set formatting for paragraphs by selecting them, and then using one of the buttons on the formatting toolbar or one of the keyboard shortcuts. *See also* "Keyboard Shortcuts." To apply the format to a single paragraph, just place the insertion point anywhere in the paragraph.

Using the Format Painter

You can use the Format Painter to quickly copy character and paragraph formatting from one bit of text to another. The Format Painter works only if you already have some text formatted the way you like. Follow these steps to use the Format Painter:

1. Highlight the text with the format you want to copy.

2. Click the Format Painter button on the Standard toolbar.

3. Point to the text that you want to copy the format to, then press and hold the mouse button and drag the pointer over the text. Word automatically formats the new text to look just like the previously formatted text.

If you want to use the Format Painter to format two or more sections of text, highlight the text you want to use as your template and then double-click the Format Painter button. The Format Painter continuously formats text that you highlight until you either press a keyboard key, double-click the mouse again, or click the Format Painter button again.

If you really like keyboard shortcuts, move the insertion point to the text that has the format you want to copy and press Ctrl+Shift+C. Then, highlight the text you want to apply the format to and press Ctrl+Shift+V.

Headers and Footers

To add a header or footer to a document, follow these steps:

1. Choose View⇨Header and Footer.

The Header and Footer toolbar appears, along with the header of the current page. (If you haven't yet created a header for the document, the header area is blank.)

2. To switch between headers and footers, click the Header and Footer button in the toolbar.

3. Type the text of your header or footer in the header or footer area, formatting the text any way you want.

You can use the Insert Auto Text button to insert information that is commonly used in a header or footer, such as the page number, the author's name, the filename, and so on.

4. Click the other buttons in the Header and Footer toolbar to add the page numbers or the date or time. Here's what each button does:

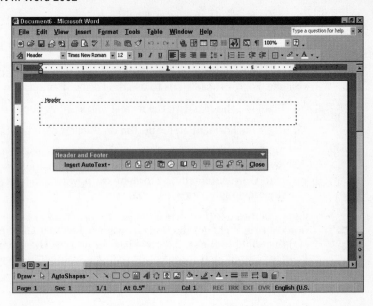

Button	What It Does
	Inserts the number of the current page.
	Inserts the total number of pages in the document.
	Enables you to specify a format for page numbers.
	Inserts the date.
	Inserts the time.
	Opens the Page Setup dialog box with the Layout tab appearing on top. This allows you to control the layout of the headers and footers of the document.
	This hides the document text from your screen while you are working with your headers and footers.
	Sets up the same header or footer as you used previously in the document. This is useful if you need to have different headers or footers in the same document.
	Switches between the header and footer.
	Shows the previous header or footer in the document.

Button	What It Does
	Shows the next header or footer in the document.
Close	Closes the Header and Footer toolbar.

5. Click the Close button after you finish adding a header or footer.

For more information, see *Word 2002 For Dummies*.

Hyperlinks

A *hyperlink* is a bit of text or graphic on a document that you can click to display another document. The hyperlink may lead to another location in the current document, another Office document, or a page on the World Wide Web.

To create a hyperlink in a Web document, follow these steps:

1. Type the text that you want to use for the hyperlink.

If you prefer, you can insert a picture instead.

2. Select the text or picture that you want to use for the hyperlink.

3. Choose Insert⇔Hyperlink to call up the Insert Hyperlink dialog box.

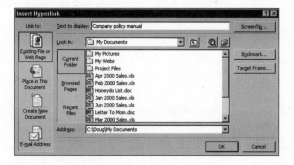

4. Use the controls in the Insert Hyperlink dialog box to locate the file that you want to link to.

To link to an Office document, use the Look In list box to locate the folder that contains the document, then click the document to select it.

To link to a Web page, type the Internet address of the Web page in the Address field. For example, type http://www.dummies.com to link to the ...*For Dummies* Web page.

To link to a location in the current document, click the Place in This Document icon in the Link To section at the left side of the Insert Hyperlink dialog box, then select the document location to link to.

5. Click OK.

Keyboard Shortcuts

The following tables list the most useful Word keyboard shortcuts.

Keyboard shortcuts for editing

Shortcut	What It Does
Ctrl+X	Cuts text to the Clipboard.
Ctrl+C	Copies text to the Clipboard.
Ctrl+V	Pastes text from the Clipboard.
Ctrl+Z	Undoes the most recent command.
Ctrl+Y	Redoes an undone command.
Ctrl+Del	Deletes from the insertion point to the end of the word.
Ctrl+Backspace	Deletes from the insertion point to the start of the word.
Ctrl+F	Finds text.
Ctrl+H	Replaces occurrences of one text string with another text string.
Ctrl+A	Selects the entire document.

Keyboard shortcuts for formatting characters

Shortcut	Button	What It Does
Ctrl+B	**B**	**Bolds** text.
Ctrl+I	*I*	*Italicizes* text.
Ctrl+U	U	Underlines text (continuous).
Ctrl+Shift+W		Underlines words.

Shortcut	Button	What It Does
Ctrl+Shift+D		Double-underlines text.
Ctrl+Shift+A		Sets the font to all caps.
Ctrl+Shift+K		Sets the font to small caps.
Ctrl+=		Uses subscript font.
Ctrl+Shift+=		Uses superscript font.
Ctrl+Shift+H		Hides the text.
Shift+F3		Changes from uppercase to lowercase and vice versa.
Ctrl+Shift+*		Displays nonprinting characters.
Ctrl+K		Inserts a hyperlink.
Ctrl+Shift+F	Times New Roman	Changes font.
Ctrl+Shift+P	9	Changes point size.
Ctrl+]		Increases size by one point.
Ctrl+[		Decreases size by one point.
Ctrl+Shift+>		Increases size to next available size.
Ctrl+Shift+<		Decreases size to preceding available size.
Ctrl+Shift+Q		Switches to Symbol font Γρεεκ Τραγεδψ
Ctrl+Shift+Z		Removes character formatting.
Ctrl+spacebar		Removes character formatting.

Keyboard shortcuts for formatting paragraphs

Shortcut	Button	What It Does
Ctrl+L		Left-aligns a paragraph.
Ctrl+R		Right-aligns a paragraph.
Ctrl+J		Justifies a paragraph.
Ctrl+E		Centers a paragraph.

cont.

Shortcut	*Button*	*What It Does*
Ctrl+M		Increases left indent.
Ctrl+Shift+M		Reduces left indent.
Ctrl+T		Creates a hanging indent.
Ctrl+Shift+T		Reduces a hanging indent.
Ctrl+1		Single-spaces a paragraph.
Ctrl+2		Double-spaces a paragraph.
Ctrl+5		Sets line spacing to 1.5.
Ctrl+0 (zero)		Removes or sets space before a line to one line.
Ctrl+Shift+S		Applies a style.
Ctrl+Shift+N		Applies Normal style.
Ctrl+Alt+1		Applies Heading 1 style.
Ctrl+Alt+2		Applies Heading 2 style.
Ctrl+Alt+3		Applies Heading 3 style.
Ctrl+Shift+L		Applies List style.
Ctrl+Q		Removes paragraph formatting.
		Formats a numbered list.
		Formats a bullet list.

Assigning your own keyboard shortcuts

In the event that Word doesn't supply enough keyboard shortcuts to fill your needs, you can easily create your own shortcuts. You can assign your own keyboard shortcuts to styles, macros, fonts, AutoText entries, commands, and symbols. Just follow these steps:

1. Choose Tools⇨Customize to open the Customize dialog box.

2. Click on the Commands tab and click on the Keyboard button on the bottom of the dialog box.

The Customize Keyboard dialog box appears:

3. Select the command, style, macro, font, or other item that you want to create a keyboard shortcut for by using the Categories and Commands lists.

4. Click the Press New Shortcut Key box and then type the new keyboard shortcut.

5. Click the Assign button to assign the keyboard shortcut and then click the Close button.

You can quickly create a keyboard shortcut for a symbol (such as a check mark or a pointed finger) by finding it using the Insert⇨Symbol command, then clicking the Shortcut Key button in the Insert Symbol dialog box.

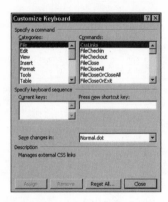

To create a keyboard shortcut for a style, first choose Format⇨Styles and Formatting to bring up the Styles and Formatting pane. Then, right-click the style, choose Modify, then click the Format button and select the Shortcut Key option from the menu that appears.

To reset all keyboard shortcuts to their Word defaults, choose Tools⇨Customize, click the Keyboard button in the Customize dialog box to summon the Customize Keyboard dialog box, and then click the Reset All button.

Mail Merging

Mail Merge is one of the most tedious of all Word tasks. Mail Merge is a three-step process. First, you create the form letter (in Wordspeak, the *main document*). Then you create a mailing list of names and addresses (the *data source*). Finally, you merge the form letter and the mailing list to create a letter for each person on your mailing list. Fortunately, Word includes a helpful Mail Merge Wizard that takes you through the entire process step by step.

To start the Mail Merge Wizard, first create a new blank document or open an existing letter. Then, choose Tools⇨Letters and Mailings⇨Mail Merge Wizard. The Wizard appears in the side pane at the right side of the document window, as shown here:

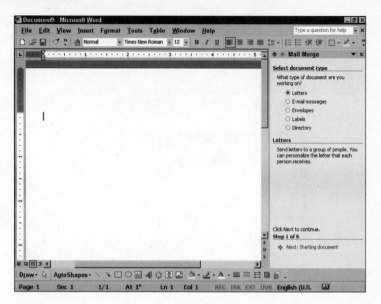

After you call up the wizard, you can follow the steps outlined in the following sections.

Creating the main document

The first Mail Merge task that the wizard helps you to accomplish is setting up your main document. Here are the steps:

1. Select the type of documents that you want to create for your mailing: letters, e-mail messages, envelopes, labels, or a directory.

2. Click Next at the bottom of the Mail Merge Wizard. The next page of the wizard appears:

3. Click the Use the Current Document option if it is not already selected.

4. Type the body of your letter. Leave out the address block and greeting line. You add those later.

5. Choose File⇨Save to save the file when you're done. Your letter should look something like the one shown here:

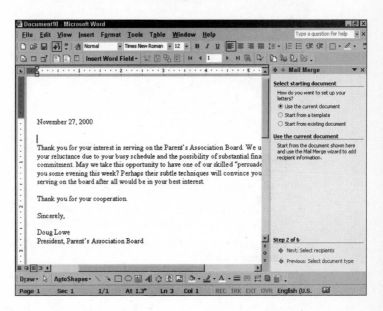

Creating an Address List

The next big step in Mail Merge is to select the recipients who will receive your letters. This step is usually the hardest part of the entire procedure, because it often involves creating an address list with the names and addresses of your recipients. Here are the bothersome steps:

1. If you haven't already done so, click Next at the bottom of the wizard to proceed to the Select Recipients step:

2. Click the Type a New List radio button, then click Create. This summons the New Address List dialog box:

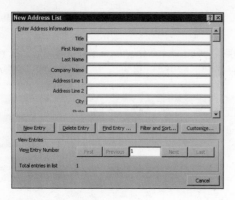

3. Type the information for a person that you want to add to the Address List. Use Tab to move from field to field or to skip over fields in which you don't want to enter any data. (You don't need to enter a value for every field.)

4. After you type all the data for the person, click the New Entry button to add that person's data to the Address List.

5. Repeat Steps 3 and 4 for each person that you want to add to the data source.

6. After you add all the names that you want to, click Close. A Save Address List dialog box appears.

7. Type a name for your address list, then click Save. The file is saved to your computer's hard drive. Then, the Mail Merge Recipients dialog box appears, as shown:

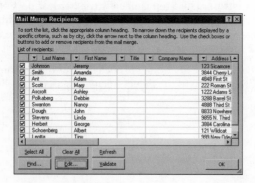

8. Click the column heading for the column that you want the list sorted by. For example, if you want the letters to print in Zip Code sequence, click the heading for the Zip Code column (you have to scroll the list to the right to see the Zip Code column),

9. Uncheck any records that you don't want to include in the mailing.

10. Click OK.

You can use the First, Previous, Next, and Last arrow buttons near the bottom of the New Address List dialog box to move forward or backward through the Address List. You can use the Previous button to call up a record you've already entered to correct a mistake if necessary.

To delete a record, use the arrow buttons at the bottom of the Data Form dialog box to move to the record that you want to delete and then click the Delete button.

The Address List feature is actually a built-in database program that is designed especially for Mail Merge. You can customize the fields that are used for each record in the Address List by clicking the Customize button. This brings up a dialog box that lets you add fields, remove existing fields, or change the order in which the Address List fields appear.

Word offers ways other than Address List to store the names and addresses for your mailings. The two most popular choices are in an Access database or in your Outlook Address book. To use names and addresses from Outlook, choose Select from Outlook Contacts in Step 2. To use an Access database (or any other database), choose Select a Different List, then locate the database in the dialog box that appears.

Inserting the address block and greeting line

After you finish adding names and addresses to the data source, it's time to finish your letter by adding the address block and greeting line. Here's the procedure:

1. Click Next at the bottom of the wizard to bring up the next set of options:

2. Position the insertion point where you want to insert the address block.

3. Click Address Block. The Insert Address Block dialog box appears.

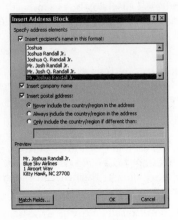

4. Choose the options that you want to use for the address block by indicating which format to use for the recipient's name, whether to use the company name, and whether to use country and region information in the address. Then click OK to insert the address block and to dismiss the Insert Address Block dialog box.

5. Position the cursor where you want the greeting line inserted.

6. Click Greeting Line to summon the Insert Greeting Line dialog box.

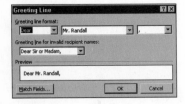

7. Choose the options that you want to use for the greeting line. Then click OK to insert the greeting line and to dismiss the Insert Greeting Line dialog box.

Here's how the letter should appear after you have inserted the address block and greeting lines:

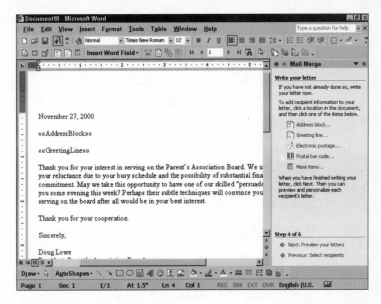

Merging the documents

After you set up the main document and the address list, you're ready for the show. Follow these simple steps to merge the main document with the data source to produce form letters:

1. Click Next to call up the next step — Preview Your Letters. The first letter in your mail merge appears on the screen.

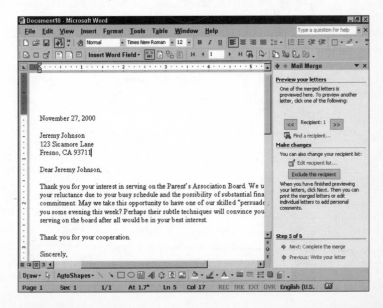

2. Click the Arrow buttons to display each of the letters in your merge. If you find a mistake in a name or address, correct the mistake directly on the letter. If you find a letter that shouldn't be included, click the Exclude This Recipient button.

3. When you have reviewed the entire mailing, click Next at the bottom of the Wizard to proceed to the final step.

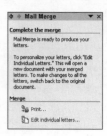

4. Click Print to print your letters.

Using the Mail Merge Toolbar

If you are an experienced Mail Merge user, you can save time by skipping the Mail Merge Wizard and jumping straight to the Mail Merge Toolbar to complete your mail merge tasks. To call up the Mail Merge Toolbar, choose Tools⇨Letters and Mailings⇨Show Mail Merge Toolbar or View⇨Toolbars⇨Mail Merge.

The following table lists the buttons that appear on the Mail Merge Toolbar. In general, you should use these buttons in sequence from left to right to complete a mail merge.

Button	*What It Does*
	Lets you choose Letters, E-mail messages, Envelopes, or Labels for the main document type
	Opens the data source
	Lets you select which names to include in the mailing and lets you determine the sort order (for example, by last name or by zip code)
	Inserts an address block
	Inserts a greeting line
	Inserts a merge field, which lets you add additional information from the data source

Button	*What It Does*
Insert Word Field ▾	Inserts a Word field, which gives you more precise control over the contents of your merged letters
« » ABC	Displays the merged data
	Highlights merged fields
	Allows you to specify which fields in a database should be used for certain mail merge functions
	Duplicates the contents of one label into all other labels on the page
◀	Goes to the first record in the data source
◀	Goes to the previous record in sequence in the data source
1	Goes to a specific record in the data source
▶	Goes to the next record in the data source
▶	Goes to the last record in the data source
	Searches for records
	Checks for merge errors
	Merges the main document and data source, placing the result in a new document
	Merges the main document and data source, sending the result directly to the printer
	Merges the main document and data source, e-mailing the resulting letters
	Merges the main document and data source, faxing the results

Numbered Lists

To create a numbered list, follow this procedure:

1. Type one or more paragraphs that you want to number.

2. Select all the paragraphs that you want to number.

3. Click the Numbering button on the Formatting toolbar.

If you add or delete a paragraph in the middle of the numbered list, Word renumbers the paragraphs to preserve the order. If you add a paragraph to the end of the list, Word assigns the next number in sequence to the new paragraph.

The Numbering button works like a toggle: Click the button once to add numbers to paragraphs; click the button again to remove them. To remove numbering from a numbered paragraph, place the insertion point anywhere in the paragraph and click the Numbering button. To remove numbering from an entire list, select all the paragraphs in the list and click the Numbering button.

If you insert a non-numbered paragraph in the middle of a numbered list, Word cuts the list into two parts and begins numbering from one again for the second list. If you simply turn off numbering for one of the paragraphs in a list, however, Word suspends the numbering for that paragraph and picks up where the sequence left off for the next numbered paragraph.

For more advanced numbering options, choose Format⇨Bullets and Numbering and then choose the Numbered or Outline Numbered tabs.

Replacing Text

You can choose Edit⇨Replace to replace all occurrences of one bit of text with other text. Here's the procedure:

1. Press Ctrl+Home to get to the top of the document. If you skip this step, the search-and-replace operation starts at the position of the insertion point.

2. Choose Edit⇨Replace or press Ctrl+H to open the Find and Replace dialog box with the Replace tab active.

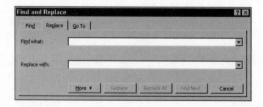

3. Type the text that you want to find in the Find What box and then type the text that you want to substitute in the Replace With box.

4. Click the Find Next button. After Word finds the text, the program highlights the text on-screen.

5. Click the Replace button to replace the text.

6. Repeat Steps 4 and 5 until you finish searching the document. Word displays a message to tell you when it's finished.

As for the Find command, you can click the More button to display additional options such as Match Case, Find Whole Words Only, Use Wildcards, Sounds Like, and Find All Word Forms options. *See also* "Finding Text."

If you're absolutely positive that you want to replace all occurrences of your Find What/Replace With text, click the Replace All button. This feature automatically replaces all occurrences of the text. The only problem is that you're bound to encounter at least one spot where you don't want to make the replacement. Replacing the word *mit* with *glove*, for example, changes *Smith* to *Sgloveh*. (And no, Sgloveh is *not* the Czechoslovakian form of the name Smith.)

If you do click the Replace All button, Word displays an informative message at the end of the replacement procedure, indicating how many replacements were made. If this number seems unreasonable to you (for example, you thought the document contained only three occurrences of the word "warthog," but Word says that it made 257 changes), choose Edit⇨Undo to undo all the replacements in one fell swoop.

Reviewing Changes

Word has the built-in ability to track any changes that you or anyone else makes while you are editing a document so you can review the changes later.

To track changes in a Word document, choose the Tools⇨Track Changes command. When you work with a document that has the Track Changes option set, the Reviewing toolbar is automatically displayed. The following table describes the buttons in this toolbar.

Button	What It Does
Final ▼	Lets you choose whether to display the final version of a document, the final version with changes, the original version with changes, or just the original version
⇥	Goes to the next revision

cont.

Button	What It Does
	Goes to the previous revision
	Accepts a change or all changes
	Rejects a change or all changes
	Inserts a comment
	Turns tracking on or off
	Shows or hides the reviewing pane, where you can see revisions and comments

Selecting Text

You can select text in a document in many ways by using the mouse or the keyboard.

Selecting text by using the mouse

Here are the common mouse actions for selecting text:

- Drag the mouse over the text that you want to select.

- Click the mouse at the start of a block of text, press and hold Shift, and then click again at the end of the block. This procedure selects everything between the clicks.

- Double-click to select a single word.

- Triple-click to select an entire paragraph.

- Press and hold Ctrl and then click to select an entire sentence.

- Press and hold Alt and then drag the mouse to select any rectangular area of text.

- Click the selection bar (the invisible vertical area to the left of the text) to select a line.

- Double-click the selection bar to select an entire paragraph.

Selecting text by using the keyboard

You can use the following keyboard techniques to select text:

✔ Place the cursor at the beginning of the text that you want to select, press and hold Shift, and then move the cursor to the end of the text that you want to select by using the cursor-control arrow keys. Release Shift after you select the desired text.

✔ Press Ctrl+A to select the entire document.

✔ Press F8 and then press any key to extend the selection to the next occurrence of that key's character. For example, to select text from the current location to the end of a sentence, press F8 and then press the period key.

You can keep extending the selection by pressing other keys. For example, if you press the period key again, the selection is extended to the next period. To stop extending the selection, press Esc.

Styles

Styles are one of the best ways to improve your word processing efficiency. A *style* is a collection of paragraph and character formats that you can apply to text in one fell swoop. Styles are most commonly used for headings. By using a style to format your headings, you can make sure that all headings are formatted in the same way. And you can quickly change the appearance of all headings by simply changing the style.

Applying a style

To apply a style to a paragraph, follow these steps:

1. Put the cursor in the paragraph that you want to format.

| Normal ▾ | *2.* Select the style that you want from the style box on the Formatting toolbar. The *style box* is the first drop-down list box control on the Formatting toolbar.

To apply a style to two or more adjacent paragraphs, just select a range of text that includes all the paragraphs that you want to format. Then select the style.

If the style that you want doesn't appear in the style list, press and hold Shift and then click the down arrow next to the style box. Word lists only the most commonly used styles if you don't hold down Shift.

For more information on styles, see *Word 2002 For Dummies.*

Creating a style

To create a new style, follow these steps:

1. Tweak a paragraph until the text is formatted just the way you want. Set the font and size, line spacing, before and after spacing, and indentation. Also set tabs and any other formatting you want, such as bullets or numbers. You can set these formatting options by using either the controls on the Formatting toolbar or the commands on the Format menu.

2. Click anywhere in the paragraph that you want to base the style on and then press Ctrl+Shift+S or click the style box on the Formatting toolbar.

3. Type a descriptive name for the style.

4. Press Enter to add the style to the list of styles for the document.

Alternatively, you can choose Format⇨Styles and Formatting to summon the Styles and Formatting task pane, then click the New Style button. A New Style dialog box appears, enabling you to set all the formatting options for a new style.

For more information, see *Word 2002 For Dummies.*

Using the Styles and Formatting task pane

A different way to work with styles is to summon the Styles and Formatting task pane by choosing the Format⇨Styles and Formatting command. As the figure shows, the Styles and Formatting task pane lists the styles that are available to your document. You can apply a style by selecting the text that you want formatted with the style, then clicking the style in the Styles and Formatting task pane.

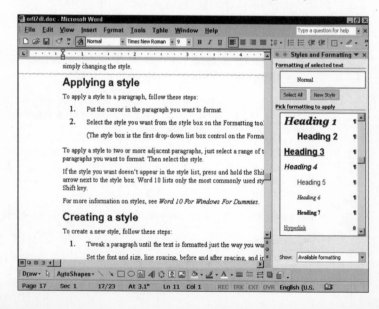

Table of Contents

To create a table of contents (or TOC), make sure that you format your document's headings by using Word's built-in heading styles (Heading 1, Heading 2, and Heading 3). If you use the heading styles, creating a table of contents is easy. Here's the procedure:

1. Move the insertion point to the place in your document where you want the table of contents to appear.

2. Choose Insert⇨Reference⇨Index and Tables.

   The Index and Tables dialog box appears.

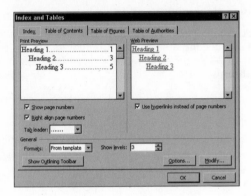

3. Click the Table of Contents tab.

4. Pick the Table of Contents style that you want from the Formats list.

5. Play with the other controls to fine-tune the table of contents.

   The following table describes the other controls of this dialog box.

Option	What It Does
Show page numbers	Clear this check box if you want the TOC to show the document's outline without page numbers.
Right align page numbers	Clear this check box if you want the page numbers to be placed next to the corresponding text rather than at the right margin.
Tab leader	Select the tab leader style that you want to use.
Formats	Select the built-in formatting option you want to use for your TOC.

cont.

Option	What It Does
Show levels	Use this control to set the amount of detail included in the table.
Use hyperlinks instead page numbers	For Web documents, place a hyperlink in the of Table of Contents for each heading.

6. Click OK. Word inserts the TOC into your document at the insertion point.

If the table of contents looks like {TOC \o "1-3" \p " "}, choose Tools⇨Options to open the Options dialog box, click the View tab, and click the Field codes check box to remove the check mark. Click OK, and the table appears as it should.

If you edit a document after creating a table of contents, you can update the table of contents to make sure that its page numbers are still correct. Select the table by clicking anywhere in it with the mouse and then press F9.

Tables

Tables enable you to organize information into a spreadsheet-like grid. You can create tables in Word in two ways: The old fashioned way, by using the Table⇨Insert Table command, or the newer way, which uses a fancy command called Draw Table.

Tables a la the Insert Table command

Word includes a friendly Insert Table command that enables you to create tables by using any of several predefined formats. Here is the procedure:

1. Position the insertion point where you want to insert the table into your document.

2. Choose Table⇨Insert⇨Table. An Insert Table dialog box appears.

3. Select the size of the table by setting the Number of columns and Number of rows text boxes.

4. Click the AutoFormat button to open the Table AutoFormat dialog box.

5. Choose the format that you want to use for the table from the list of Table Styles.

6. Specify any other options that you want to apply to the table, such as whether to use special formatting for the first row or column.

7. Click OK to close the Table AutoFormat dialog box and then click OK to create the table.

Want a faster way to insert a table into your document? Simply click the Insert Table button. This produces a drop-down box that shows a grid of columns and rows. Drag your cursor diagonally across the drop-down box to highlight the number of rows and columns that you want in your table. When you release the mouse button, your table is inserted at the current cursor position.

After you create a table, you can type data into its cells by clicking the desired cell and typing the data. You can use the arrow keys to move from cell to cell in any direction you want, or you can press Tab to move to the next cell in the table.

Tables via the Draw Table command

The Draw Table command is a feature that enables you to draw complicated tables on-screen by using a simple set of drawing tools. The Draw Table command is ideal for creating tables that aren't merely a simple grid of rows and columns, but instead boast a complex conglomeration of cells, in which some cells span more than one row and others span more than one column. With the Draw Table command, you can create this type of table with just a few clicks of the mouse. Here's the procedure:

1. Choose Table⇨Draw Table or click the Tables and Borders button on the Standard toolbar. You can also get to this toolbar by clicking View⇨Toolbars⇨Tables and Borders. Word switches into Page Layout View (if you aren't already there) and opens the Tables and Borders toolbar.

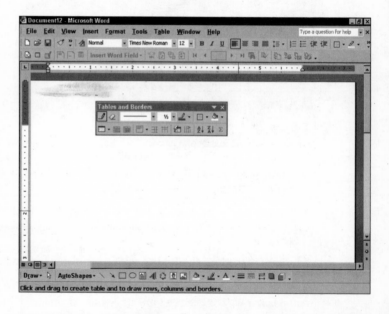

2. Draw the overall shape of the table by dragging the mouse to create a rectangular boundary for the table. Point the mouse where you want one of the corners of the table to be and then press and hold the mouse button while dragging the rectangle to the opposite corner. After you release the mouse button, a table with a single cell appears:

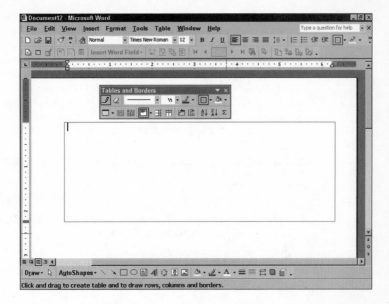

3. Carve the table up into smaller cells. To split the table into two rows, for example, point the mouse somewhere along the left edge of the table, press and hold the mouse button, and then drag a line across the table to the right edge. After you release the mouse, the table splits into two rows:

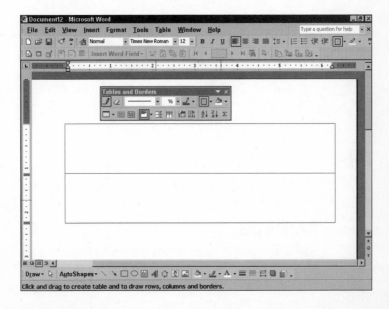

You can continue to carve up the table into smaller and smaller cells. For each slice, point the mouse at one edge of where you want the new cell to begin and drag the mouse to the other edge. If you want to change the line size or style drawn for a particular segment, you can use the line style and size drop-down controls in the Tables and Borders toolbar. You can change the style of a line that you've already drawn by tracing over the line with a new style. The following figure shows some of the possibilities available to create your table:

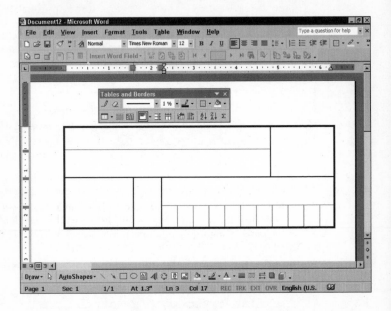

4. After you finish creating your table, click the Tables and Borders button again to close the Tables and Borders toolbar. You can then type data into any of the table's cells by clicking the cell to select it and typing the data.

Tabs

The following sections list the most common procedures for working with tabs.

Setting tabs

Here's the procedure for setting tabs by using the ruler, which sits on top of the document window. (If the ruler isn't visible, use the View⇨Ruler command to reveal it.) Follow these steps:

1. Type some text that you want to line up with tab stops.

2. Select the paragraph or paragraphs that you want to set tabs for.

3. Click the ruler at each spot where you want a new tab stop. A little icon representing the tab will be placed at each spot you click on the ruler.

4. Adjust the settings.

5. Return to your text and add the tabs at the appropriate places.

To adjust a tab setting, just use the mouse to grab the tab marker in the ruler and slide the tab to the new location. (If you can't find the ruler, choose View➪Ruler.) After you release the mouse button, text in the currently selected paragraphs adjusts to the new tab position.

Default tab stops are located at every half-inch in the ruler. Each time you create a new tab stop, however, Word deletes all default tab stops to the left of the new tab stop. In other words, default tab stops continue to exist only to the right of new tab stops that you create.

Word enables you to create four types of tab alignments: *left*, *center*, *right*, and *decimal*. To change the type of tab that you created as you click the ruler, click the Tab Alignment button at the far-left edge of the ruler. Each time you click this button, the picture on the button changes to indicate the alignment type, as follows:

✔ **Left tab:** Left-aligns text at the tab stop.

✔ **Center tab:** Centers text over the tab stop.

✔ **Right tab:** Right-aligns text at the tab stop.

✔ **Decimal tab:** Aligns numbers at the decimal point over the tab stop.

To remove a tab stop from the ruler, click the tab stop that you want to remove and drag the tab off the ruler. After you release the mouse button, the tab stop disappears.

To remove all tab stops quickly, choose Format➪Tabs and then click the Clear All button in the Tabs dialog box.

For more information, see *Word 2002 For Dummies.*

Creating leader tabs

Leader tabs have rows of dots instead of spaces between tab stops. (Leader tabs are common in tables of contents and indexes.) Here's the procedure for creating leader tabs:

1. Set a tab stop. *See also* "Setting tabs."

2. Choose Format⇨Tabs. The Tabs dialog box appears.

3. Choose the leader style by selecting option 2, 3, or 4 in the Leader area.

4. Click OK.

The Tabs dialog box is closed and you are returned to your document. Now, when you press Tab in the paragraph, a row of dots or a solid line appears.

For more information, see *Word 2002 For Dummies*.

Templates

Suppose that you toiled for hours on a document, and now you want to make its styles, macros, and other goodies available to other documents that you may want to create later. You can do that by creating a *template*. Then, if you create a new document based on your template, that document inherits the styles, *AutoText entries* (portions of prerecorded text that you can call up with just a few mouse clicks), macros, and text from the template. Here's how to create a template:

1. Open the document that has all the styles, AutoText, macros, and other goodies you want to save in a template.

2. Choose File⇨Save As to open the Save As dialog box.

3. In the Save As Type list box (way down at the bottom of the Save As dialog box), select Document Template as the file type.

4. In the File Name text box, type a filename for the template.

   Don't type the extension; Word takes care of that element.

5. Click the Save button to save the document as a template file.

6. Delete any unnecessary text from the file.

   Any text that you do not delete appears automatically in any new documents that you create based on the template.

7. Save the file again.

For more information, see *Word 2002 For Dummies.*

Themes

Themes are sort of like templates, in that they define fonts, styles, and other formatting elements for your documents. However, significant differences exist between the two. Themes do not automatically include macros, AutoText, or customized settings. Themes differ from templates in that they give you a unified design scheme that can include background images, fonts, bullets, horizontal lines, and other design elements. Using themes allows you to create consistently professional-looking documents, and they are especially good for Web page design.

If you don't like any of the themes that come with Word and you don't want to go through the work of creating your own, you can use themes that are available online. Simply click Help⇨Office on the Web and follow the directions to download more themes onto your computer.

Applying a theme to a document

To start your document with a theme already applied, follow these steps:

1. With the document open, select Format⇨Theme.

   The Theme dialog box opens. It doesn't matter whether you've already worked on the document or whether you're just starting. Just make sure that you can see an active cursor within the document screen and that no text is highlighted.

2. The Theme dialog box shows you a list of available themes in the Choose a Theme window on the left, and the window on the right displays a sample of the theme that is currently selected. Scroll through the list and look at the samples until you find one you like.

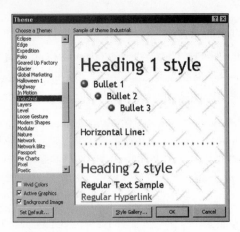

3. In the lower-left corner are three checkboxes that allow you to refine your control of the theme. These three boxes are Vivid Colors, Active Graphics, and Background Image. Play with turning these three boxes on and off to see how they affect the look of your document, and until you find the look you want.

4. Click OK.

You can mix and match themes with predetermined styles. At the bottom of the Theme dialog box is the Style Gallery button. If you click this button, the Style Gallery dialog box opens. From this dialog box, you can choose different styles and see what your document will look like using that style with the theme you've chosen. Nifty, eh?

Changing the default theme

Word has a default theme that it applies to all documents when they are first open. You can change this default so that a new theme always appears whenever you open a new Word document. To do this:

1. Click Format➪Theme to open the Theme dialog box.

2. Determine the theme that you want in the same manner as described in Applying a Theme, and click the Set Default button. A dialog box appears, asking whether you want to set a new default theme for new documents.

3. If you really want to do this, click Yes.

4. Click OK in the Theme dialog box. From now on, every new Word document you create has that theme applied to it, until you decide to change it.

Web Page Wizard

Do you want to make yourself known on the World Wide Web with your own Web page, but are afraid that you're not enough of a geek for the complex HTML programming? Fear not! Word comes with a slick Web Page Wizard that can automatically create several different types of Web documents based on options that you select. Trust me — anyone who can create a Word document can create a Web site using the Web Page Wizard. To use the wizard, follow these steps:

1. Choose File⇨New to summon the New Document pane.

2. Click General Templates in the New From Template section of the New Document pane to summon the Templates dialog box. Click the Web Pages tab, click Web Page Wizard, and then click OK. The Web Page Wizard dialog box appears.

   If you have recently used the Web Page Wizard, you'll find the Web Page Wizard listed near the bottom of the New Documents pane. In that case, just click Web Page Wizard in the New Documents pane to summon the wizard directly, without trudging through the Templates dialog box.

3. Click the Title and Location button on the left side of the window or click Next to move to the next screen on the list. This allows you to give your site a title (which also functions as its file name) and the location where you want to save it on your system.

4. When you have entered that information, click the Next button to proceed to the next page of the wizard.

5. Choose how you want your navigation links to be displayed on your page. You have three options, which are

   • **Vertical frame.** This divides your screen with a vertical line. On the left are the links, which, when clicked, show the content on the right side of the screen.

   • **Horizontal frame.** Divides the screen into a top half and a bottom half. The links appear on the top, and the content is displayed in the bottom half.

   • **Separate page.** With this option, a separate page is displayed when you click a link.

6. After you've made your choice, click the Next button. The next screen shows the Add Pages portion of the Web Page Wizard. With this feature, you can select what types of documents are associated with your Web page. You can use Add New Blank

Page for plain text, Add Template Page for specific Web templates (such as FAQ, Tables of Contents, or columns), and Add Existing File, which allows you to add any document from your computer system.

7. Select the pages that you want to include and then click Next. The Organize Pages feature allows you to determine the order in which the individual pages appear on your Web site. Simply highlight one of the pages and then click either the Move Up or the Move Down button to position it where you want. Repeat with the different pages until everything is in the desired order.

8. Click Next. A screen appears which allows you to apply a visual theme to your document or keep it simple with a plain white background. *See also* "Themes."

9. After you've chosen a theme, click Next again. That's it! Your Web page is organized and ready for you to enter the information on it.

10. Click the Finish button, and the document appears on your screen.

For even more complete knowledge of Web sites and how to build them, please look at *Word 2002 For Dummies*.

Excel 2002

Excel is the bean counter of Microsoft Office XP. It enables you to create spreadsheets that can perform meticulous calculations with uncanny accuracy. This part covers the basics of using Excel. If you're interested in going beyond the basics, you can find more information in *Excel 2002 For Dummies,* by Greg Harvey, published by Hungry Minds, Inc.

In this part . . .

AutoFormatting

You can efficiently create an attractively formatted worksheet by using the AutoFormat feature, which applies predefined formatting to your worksheet. Here's how:

1. **Create your worksheet.** The AutoFormat feature works best when the first row and the first column of the worksheet contain headings and the last row contains totals, because many of the AutoFormats apply special formatting to the first row and first column. The last column of the worksheet may also contain totals, but it doesn't have to. The AutoFormats work whether the last column contains totals or not. They also work if the first row and first column don't contain headings, but you may have to remove the special formatting from the first row and first column.

2. **Highlight the entire range of worksheet cells containing the data that you want to format,** as shown in the following figure:

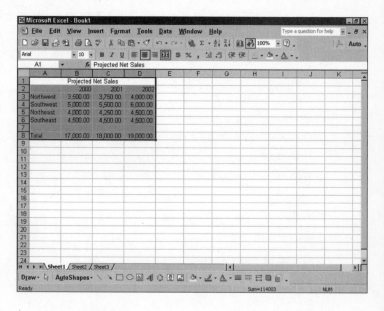

3. **Choose Format⇨AutoFormat.** The AutoFormat dialog box appears, as shown in the following figure:

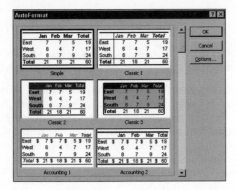

4. Select the table format of your choice from the list shown in the dialog box.

5. Click OK. Excel applies the selected AutoFormat to your worksheet, as shown in the following figure:

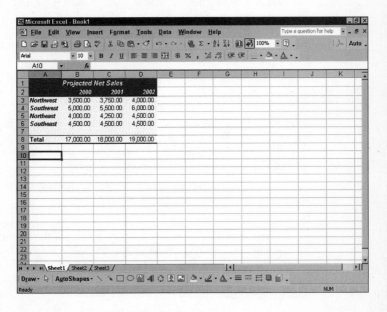

If you don't like the formatting applied by the AutoFormat, press Ctrl+Z, choose Edit ⇨Undo, or click the Undo button to undo the AutoFormat operation.

AutoSum

AutoSum is one of Excel's handiest features: It lets you quickly create formulas that add up the values in a column or row of data.

 To use AutoSum, first create a row or column of data that you want to add up. For example, if you want to add up sales for each month of the year, create a row or column with monthly sales in each cell. Then, select the first empty cell below the column or to the right of the row. Click the AutoSum button (shown in the margin). Excel attempts to determine the correct range for the sum, then inserts a Sum function in the cell. Press Enter to accept the Sum function.

 Although Excel can usually determine the correct range for the Sum function, sometimes its estimate is a cell or two off. If so, use your mouse to adjust the range proposed for the Sum function before you press Enter.

 With Excel, you can now use the AutoSum button for additional functions: Average, Count, Max, and Min. Instead of clicking the AutoSum button, click the arrow located to the right of the AutoSum button. Then, choose the function that you want to use from the menu that appears.

Borders

You can add borders around any cell in your worksheet. The border can appear on the top, bottom, left, or right edge of the cell. By mixing and matching borders on adjacent cells, you can create many different types of border effects.

 The easiest way to add borders to cells is to use the new Borders Toolbar. Just follow these steps:

1. Click the Borders button on the Formatting toolbar (shown in the margin), then choose Draw Borders from the menu that appears. The Borders toolbar appears, as shown in the figure:

 If you can't find the Borders button, click the down-arrow at the right end of the Formatting toolbar to reveal additional buttons. Or, if you prefer to work with menus, you can call up the Borders toolbar by choosing View⇨Toolbars⇨Borders.

2. Move the mouse pointer to the spot where you want the border to start, press and hold the mouse button, and drag the mouse to where you want the border to end. When you release the mouse button, a border is added.

    If you drag the mouse over a range of cells, a border is added around the cells.

3. If you make a mistake, click the Erase Border button (shown in the margin) and then click the line that you want to erase.

4. When you're finished drawing lines, click the Close button in the top-right corner of the Borders toolbar.

If you want to create a grid, click the arrow to the right of the Draw Border button and then choose Draw Border Grid from the menu that appears.

You can use the Line Style drop-down list to choose a different line style for your borders. The choices include a medley of dashed lines, double lines, and solid lines of varying thickness.

To change the line color, click the Line Color button and select the color that you want to use.

Centering Text Over Several Columns

You may frequently want to center text over several columns. For example, suppose that you put projected net sales for the years 2000, 2001, and 2002 in columns B, C, and D, respectively. Then you put actual net sales for 2000, 2001, and 2002 in columns E, F, and G. For organizational and aesthetic reasons, you probably want to place a Projected Net Sales heading centered over the projected net sales columns and an Actual Net Sales heading centered over the actual net sales columns.

You can accomplish this effect by merging cells from the three columns to create a single cell that spans several columns. Here is the procedure:

1. Move the cell pointer to the leftmost cell in the range of columns over which you want to center the text. For example, if you want text centered over the range B2:D2, move the cell pointer to cell B2. *See also* "Referencing Spreadsheet Cells," if the notation B2:D2 confuses you.

2. Enter the text that you want to center into the cell you have selected. Press Enter when you have finished typing the text.

3. Highlight the range of cells where you want the text centered.

4. Click the Merge and Center button (shown in the margin). The result should look like the example shown in the following figure. (In this example, both the Projected Net Sales and the Actual Net Sales headings are centered.)

If you change your mind and don't want to center the text across columns, highlight the merged cell and click the Merge and Center button again. The merged cells will be restored to individual cells, and the text will be returned to the cell you originally typed it into.

Charting

Excel offers so many charting capabilities that I could write an entire *Quick Reference* just on charting. Here's the short procedure for quickly creating a simple chart:

1. Select the cells that contain the data on which you want to base a chart.

2. Click the ChartWizard button on the Standard toolbar. The Chart Wizard comes to life, as shown in the following figure:

3. From the Chart Type list on the Standard Types tab, select the type of chart that you want to create. For each chart type, you can choose from several sub-types. To see a preview of how the selected data appears charted with a particular chart type, select that chart type from the list and click and hold the mouse button on the Click and Hold to View Sample button.

4. Click the Next button.

5. Check the range shown in the Data Range box to verify that the range listed is the range that you want to chart.

TIP

The Chart Wizard initially assumes that the data you are trying to chart is grouped by row. In other words, the first row of the range contains the first series of values, the second row contains the second series, and so on. If this isn't the case, you can click the Columns radio button so that the data is grouped by column, with the first data series in the first column of the range, the second series in the second column, and so on.

6. Click the Next button. The Chart Wizard asks for chart options, as shown in the following figure:

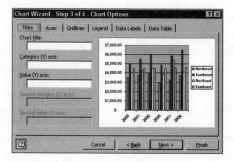

7. Add any optional features to your chart by filling in the text boxes and setting various option buttons that appear on the Chart Options version of the Chart Wizard dialog box. Notice that the Chart Options dialog box has six tabs that display various charting options. Be sure to check the settings on all six tabs before proceeding. For example, you can include a title for the chart by typing a title into the Chart Title text box.

The changes that you make to the settings on the Chart Options dialog box appear in the preview area, which takes up the entire right side of the dialog box. This preview gives you an idea of how each setting affects the chart's appearance.

8. Click the Next button. The Chart Wizard displays its final dialog box.

9. Choose how you want Excel to insert your chart — as a new sheet or as an object in any sheet in the current workbook — and then click the Finish button to create the chart.

If you add the chart to an existing sheet, you probably need to drag and possibly resize the chart to its correct location and size.

After you add a chart to your spreadsheet as an object, you can summon a toolbar to your screen that allows you to continue to manipulate the chart. Do you want to play with the chart to your heart's content — without returning to the wizard to make a new chart? To open a toolbar that allows you to do so, select View⇨ Toolbars⇨Chart. Here you find buttons to change the grouping of the data, to angle your text, to add, format, or remove the legend, or even to change the chart type. You can also tweak the chart's appearance by double-clicking on various elements of the chart to bring up dialog boxes, which allow you to set formatting options.

Comments

Excel enables you to add an electronic version of those yellow sticky notes to your worksheets. You can use this feature as a reminder to yourself and others who may use the worksheet. For example, suppose you need to post a reminder about why you created a formula the way you did or where you got a particular number that you entered into the worksheet. Just follow these steps:

1. Click the cell that you want to add the note to.

2. Choose Insert⇨Comment or press Shift+F2. A balloon-style box appears.

3. Type anything you want in the box. The following figure illustrates a typical comment:

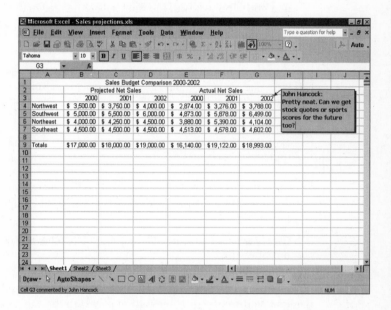

4. Click anywhere outside the comment balloon. The comment balloon disappears, and Excel adds a colored marker to the top-right corner of the cell to indicate that a comment is attached to that cell.

To access the comment later, simply point to the cell, and the comment balloon appears. The balloon disappears after you move the mouse pointer away from the cell.

To delete a comment, right-click the cell and choose Delete Comment from the pop-up menu that appears.

Conditional Formatting

Conditional formatting enables you to format a cell or range of cells to make special formatting dependent upon the value or formula in that cell. In a sales worksheet, for example, you may want the cell that contains your sales total to be italicized if it meets your sales quota.

You can create two basic types of conditions:

- A *cell-value condition* compares the value of the cell with a value that you supply or with the value of another cell in the worksheet. For example, you can create a condition that applies special formatting if the value of the cell is greater than 20,000 or if the value of the cell is equal to the value of cell A4.

- A *formula condition* is more complicated: It enables you to type any valid Excel formula. The conditional formatting is applied if the formula evaluates to True. For example, you can create a condition that applies special formatting if the formula =C>C11 is true. In other words, the conditional formatting is used if the value of cell C is greater than the value of cell C11. (Remember that formulas always have to start with an equal sign.)

Follow these steps to set up conditional formatting:

1. Highlight the cell or range of cells that you want conditional formatting added to.

2. Click Format⇨Conditional Formatting. The following dialog box appears:

3. In the drop-down list box on the left, select whether you want to create a cell-value condition or a formula condition.

4. If you are creating a formula condition, type the formula in the text box that's provided and skip the rest of this step. If you are creating a cell-value condition, use the drop-down list box in the middle of the Conditional Formatting dialog box to indicate the type of comparison that you want to make. (The choices are Between, Not Between, Equal To, Not Equal To, Greater Than, Less Than, Greater Than or Equal To, and Less

Than or Equal To.) Then type the value that you want to use
for the comparison in the text box. For example, this figure
shows a condition that applies formatting if the value of the
cell is greater than or equal to 19,000:

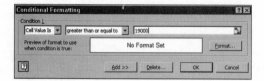

You can include cell references in the comparison value text
box. For example, type =B4 to use the value of cell B4 for the
comparison.

5. After you have set the cell value or formula, click the Format
button to summon the Format Cells dialog box, shown in the
figure.

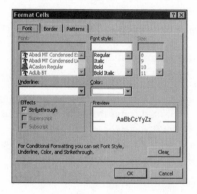

6. Apply the formatting that you want and click OK. You can
change the font, style, point size, color, border, and background shading for the cell.

7. Click OK to apply the conditional format.

You can specify as many as three conditions when you use conditional formatting. To create additional conditions, click the Add
button that appears at the bottom of the Conditional Formatting
dialog box. The following figure shows Conditional Formatting with
two conditions applied — the first condition formats the cell in
Bold Italic if the cell value is greater than 17,000, and the second
condition formats the cell in Italic if the value is greater than 15,000.

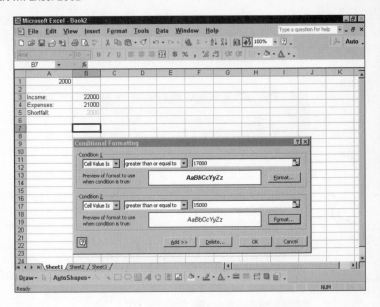

When you use more than one condition, Excel considers the conditions one at a time. As soon as one of the conditions is true, the formatting for that condition is applied and any remaining conditions are ignored. This can trip you up if you're not careful. For example, suppose you set up two conditions: The first condition formats the cell in Italic if the value is greater than 17,000, and the second condition changes the font color to red if the cell value is greater than 15,000. If the actual cell value is 20,000, will the text be displayed in red italic? The answer is no, because after the greater than 17,000 condition is met, the remaining conditions are ignored. So even though 20,000 is greater than 15,000, the second condition is never considered, so the text color doesn't change to red.

Errors

Excel automatically checks your worksheets for common types of errors, including errors in cell formulas. If Excel finds an error in a cell, the cell is marked with a little green triangle in the top-left corner of the cell.

When you click a cell that has an error, an error icon appears to the right of the cell (as shown in the margin). You can then click this icon to see a description of the error, as shown in the following figure:

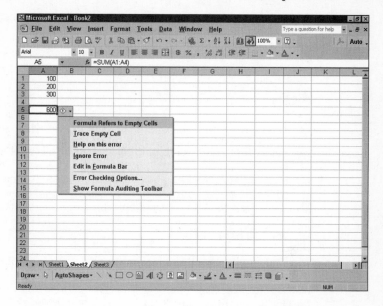

In this example, Excel informs me that the formula for cell A5, which is =SUM(A1:A4), may be an error because cell A4 is empty. The pop-up error menu gives you choices on how to deal with the error: You can edit the cell to correct the error, ignore the error, or find out more information about the error.

You can control the type of automatic error checking that Excel does by choosing the Tools⇨Options command and then clicking the Error Checking tab. Here you can disable specific types of error checks. For example, you can check for functions that refer to empty cells or you can use dates that have two-digit rather than four-digit years.

Finding Lost Data

You can choose Edit⇨Find to find text anywhere in a worksheet. Just follow these steps:

1. Press Ctrl+Home to move to the top of the worksheet. This step is optional; if you omit it, the search starts at the current cell.

2. Use the Edit⇨Find command or press Ctrl+F to summon the Find and Replace dialog box.

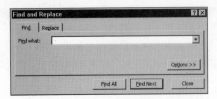

3. Type the text that you want to find in the Find What text box.

4. Click the Find Next button. Excel highlights the cell that contains the text that you're looking for after it finds the cell. The Find and Replace dialog box remains on-screen so that you can click Find Next to find yet another occurrence of the text. After Excel finds the last occurrence of the text, it resumes its search again from the top. This process goes on forever, until you bail out by clicking Close or pressing Esc.

The Find and Replace dialog box offers several options for controlling the search. These options aren't immediately visible in the Find and Replace dialog box, but you can call them up by clicking the Options button.

The following table describes the Find options:

Option	What It Does
Within	Indicates whether you want to search the entire workbook or just the current sheet.
Search	Indicates whether you want to search by rows or columns.
Look In	Indicates whether you want to search cell values, formulas, or comments attached to cells.
Match Case	Finds only text with the case (uppercase and lowercase letters) that matches the search text that you type.
Match Entire Cells Contents	Finds text only if the entire cell entry matches the Find What text.

You can use the following wildcard characters in the Find what text box:

✔ ? finds a single occurrence of any character. For example, **f?t** finds *fat* and *fit*.

✔ * finds any combination of characters. For example, **b*t** finds any combination of characters that begins with *b* and ends with *t*, such as *bat, bait, ballast,* and *bacteriologist.*

If you find the text that you're looking for and decide that you want to replace it with something else, click the Replace tab at the top of the Find and Replace dialog box.

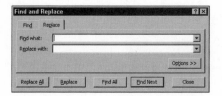

You can then type replacement text in the Replace With text box, and then click Replace to replace a single occurrence of the Find text, or Replace All to replace the Find text wherever it appears in the document.

You can find all occurrences of your search text by clicking Find All instead of Find Next. Excel displays all of the cells that contain the search text in a list at the bottom of the Find and Replace dialog box, as shown in the figure. You can click any cell listed in the Find and Replace dialog box to go to that cell.

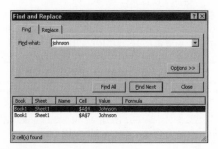

Formatting a Cell or Range of Cells

You can set formats for a cell or range of cells by using formatting keyboard shortcuts or by using the formatting controls on the Formatting toolbar. Or you can use the following procedure to apply character formats by using the Format➪Cells command:

1. Highlight the cell or cells that you want to apply the formatting to.

2. Choose Format⇨Cells or use the handy keyboard shortcut, Ctrl+1. Either way, the Format Cells dialog box appears, as shown in the following figure:

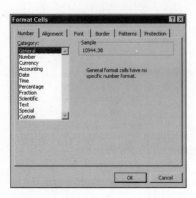

3. Play with the controls under the six tabs to set the formatting options that you want.

4. Click the OK button after you format the cells the way you want.

Functions

The following table details some common Excel functions. The program has hundreds of other functions that you can use, but these are the most common. **See also** "Function Wizard."

Command	Explanation
=ABS(number)	Returns the absolute value of *number*. *Number* is usually a cell reference, as in =ABS(B3), or the result of a calculation, such as =ABS(D19-D17).
=AVERAGE(range)	Calculates the average value of the cells in *range* by determining the sum of all the cells and then dividing the result by the number of cells in the range. Excel doesn't count blank cells, but the program does count cells that contain the value zero.

Command	*Explanation*
=COUNT(range)	Returns the number of cells in range. Excel doesn't count blank cells, but the program does count cells that contain the value zero.
=HLOOKUP(lookup_value, table_array, row_index_num)	Searches for the cell in table_array that contains the value specified by *lookup_value*. HLOOKUP searches all the cells in the first row of the range specified for *table_array*. If the function finds *lookup_value*, HLOOKUP returns the value of the corresponding cell in the row indicated by *row_index_num*. To return the value in the corresponding cell in the second row of the table, for example, specify **2** for *row_index_num*.
=IF(logical_test, value_if_true, value_if_false)	Tests the condition specified in the logical test. If the condition is true, Excel returns *value_if_true*. Otherwise, the program returns *value_if_false*.
=LOWER(text)	Converts the *text* to lowercase.
=MAXIMUM(range)	Returns the largest value in *range*.
=MEDIAN(range)	Returns the median value of the cells in *range*. If you sort the cells in order, the median value is the value in the cell that falls right in the middle of the sorted list. Half the cell values are larger than the median value, and the other half are smaller.
=MINIMUM(range)	Returns the smallest value in *range*.
=NOW()	Returns the current date and time. No arguments are required.
=PMT(rate, nper, pv)	Calculates payments for a loan. *Rate* is the interest rate per period; *nper* is the number of periods; *pv* is the present value (that is, the amount of the loan). Make sure that you specify the interest rate for each period and the total number of periods. If, for example, the annual interest rate is 12 percent and you make payments monthly, the periodic interest rate is 1 percent. Likewise, if the loan is for three years and you make payments monthly, 36 periods exist.

cont.

Command	Explanation
=PRODUCT(range)	Multiplies all the cells in the specified *range*.
=PROPER(text)	Converts the text to proper case, in which the program capitalizes the first letter of each word in *text*.
=ROUND(number, decimal places)	Rounds off the number to the specified number of decimal places. For example, =ROUND(C1,2) rounds off the value in cell C1 to two decimal places.
=SUM(range)	Adds the values of all cells in the specified *range*.
=SUMPRODUCT (range1, range2)	Multiplies each cell in *range1* by its corresponding cell in *range2* and then adds the resulting products together.
=TODAY()	Returns the current date. No arguments are required.
=UPPER(text)	Converts the *text* to uppercase.
=VLOOKUP(lookup_value, table_array, col_index_num)	Searches for the cell in *table_array* that contains the value specified by *lookup_value*. VLOOKUP searches all the cells in the first column of the range specified for table_array. If the function finds *lookup_value,* VLOOKUP returns the value of the corresponding cell in the column indicated by *col_index_num.* To return the value in the corresponding cell in the second column of the table, for example, specify **2** for *col_index_num.*

Function Wizard

The easiest way to insert a function is to use the Function Wizard. The Function Wizard asks you to select a function from one of several function categories and to complete the function by providing all the information that the function requires.

Here's the procedure, using a simple MAX function as an example:

1. Move the cell pointer to the cell in which you want to insert the function.

2. Choose Insert⇨Function or click the Insert Function button, which is located right next to the Formula Bar (the text box where you type formulas and values for cells). The Insert Function dialog box appears. The Insert Function dialog box initially lists the functions you used most recently.

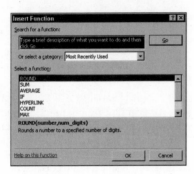

3. If the function that you want to insert in the cell appears in the list of functions, click the name of the function; otherwise, click one of the categories from the Select a Category drop-down box, then select the function from the list of functions.

If you're not sure what function to use, type a description of what you want to do in the Search for a Function text box at the top of the Insert Function dialog box, then click Go. Excel displays a list of functions that may help. For example, the figure shows the functions displayed if you search for "Calculate a mortgage payment."

4. Click OK. A dialog box appears, similar to the one in the figure:

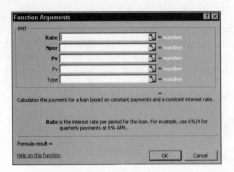

5. Read the instructions for completing the function and then type whatever entries you need to complete the function. If the function requires just a single argument, Excel uses the cell or range that was selected at the time you accessed the Function Wizard. This means that you don't need to do anything in this dialog box except to click OK. If the function requires more than one argument, you can type a value, cell reference, or range into the text boxes for the additional arguments.

Arguments that are listed in bold type are required. Arguments that are not in bold are optional; you can omit them if you don't need them for your calculation.

If you want, you can mark a cell or range of cells in the spreadsheet by clicking the button that appears to the right of the text box for the argument that you want to enter. This action returns you to the spreadsheet, where you can mark the cell or range. Press Enter to return to the Function Wizard; the range you marked appears in the text box for the argument.

6. Click OK after you complete the function. **See also** "Functions."

Moving Around Your Worksheet

You can move around a worksheet easily enough by using the mouse — just click the cell that you want to move to. **See also** "The Big Picture" for general information about moving around Office documents.

The following table summarizes the keyboard techniques that you can use for moving around a worksheet.

Shortcut	*What It Does*
Home	Moves to the beginning of the current row.
PgUp	Scrolls the window up one screen.
PgDn	Scrolls the window down one screen.
Alt+PgDn	Scrolls the window right one screen.
Alt+PgUp	Scrolls the window left one screen.
Ctrl+End	Moves to the last cell of the worksheet that contains data.
Ctrl+Home	Moves to the beginning of the worksheet.
Ctrl+← or End,←	Moves to the left of a data block.
Ctrl+→ or End,→	Moves to the right of a data block.
Ctrl+↑ or End,↑	Moves to the top of a data block.
Ctrl+↓ or End,↓	Moves to the bottom of a data block.
Ctrl+PgUp	Switches to the preceding sheet in the same workbook.
Ctrl+PgDn	Switches to the next sheet in the same workbook.
End, Home	Moves to the last cell in the worksheet that contains data.
End, Enter	Moves to the last cell in the current row that contains data.
Ctrl+G	Goes to a specific location.

Naming a Range of Cells

To make your formulas easier to understand, Excel enables you to assign meaningful names to individual cells or cell ranges. Here's the procedure for assigning a name to a cell or range of cells:

1. Select the cell or range of cells that you want to assign a name to.

2. Choose Insert⇨Name⇨Define to open the Define Name dialog box, as shown in the figure:

3. Type a name for the cell or cell range in the text box at the top of the Define Name dialog box.

Excel is picky about how you name your cells. The name can't have any spaces in it, it must use only alphanumeric characters (no symbols), and it must start with at least one letter, even if the rest of the name is numeric.

4. Click OK to close the Define Name dialog box.

To use a range name in a formula, type the name anywhere you would type a range. Instead of typing =**Sum(F4:F15)**, for example, you can type the formula =**Sum(SalesTotals)**.

To delete a range name, choose Insert⇨Name⇨Define to open the Define Name dialog box, select the range name that you want to delete from the list, and then click the Delete button.

You can quickly select a named range by either pressing F5 or choosing Edit⇨Go To to open the Go To dialog box and then double-clicking the range name in the list box.

Pivot Tables

A *pivot table* is a slick way of summarizing information stored in an Excel worksheet or an Access database. You can use pivot tables with worksheets where information is stored in rows, and where each column represents a field.

For example, suppose that you are charged with tracking the fund-raising activities of a group of students. Each row in a worksheet can represent a single fund-raising activity for a particular student, with columns for the student's name, the fund-raising activity, the amount raised, and the month in which the activity occurred. Such a worksheet may look like the example in the figure:

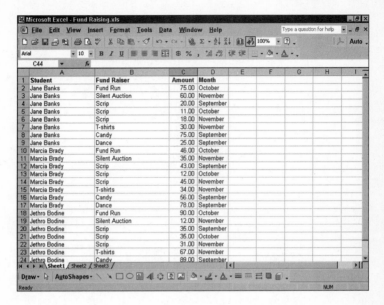

To create a pivot table from a worksheet like this, follow these steps:

1. Select a cell within the worksheet's table that you want to serve as the basis for the pivot table. The cell that you select doesn't matter, as long as the cell is within the table on the worksheet.

2. Choose Data⇨PivotTable and PivotChart Report to open the PivotTable and PivotChart Wizard, as shown in the figure:

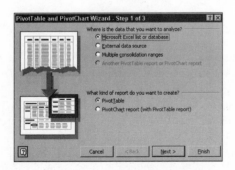

3. Leave the data source option set to Microsoft Excel List or
   Database and click the Next button to proceed. Step 2 of the
   PivotTable and PivotChart Wizard appears, as shown in the
   figure. If you selected a cell within the table before starting the
   PivotTable and PivotChart Wizard, Excel should correctly
   guess the range of cells on which to base the pivot table. If not,
   you can change it here.

4. If the correct range appears in the Range text box, click Next to
   move on to Step 3 of the PivotTable and PivotChart Wizard.

5. Determine whether you want the pivot table to be constructed
   in the same worksheet or in a new worksheet. (If you choose a
   new worksheet, it will still exist in the same file, and you can
   switch between the sheets by clicking the tabs on the bottom-
   left corner of your screen.)

6. Click the Layout button. The Layout dialog box of this wizard
   opens, as shown in the figure:

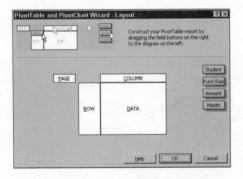

Each column in the table appears as a field button in the
PivotTable and PivotChart Wizard.

7. Pick the field that contains the data that you want to summarize and drag the button for that field into the Data area of the
   pivot table. In the Fund Raising table, for example, you drag
   the Amount field to the Data area.

8. Drag the other fields to the Row, Column, or Page areas,
   depending on how you want to summarize the data. The figure

shows how I dragged the Student button to the Column area, the Fund Raiser button to the Row area, and the Month button to the Page area.

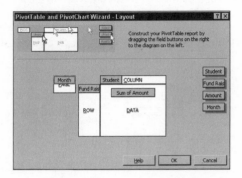

After Excel creates the pivot table, you can move these fields around to change how Excel summarizes the data.

9. Click OK to return to Step 6.

10. Click Finish to close the PivotTable and PivotChart Wizard and to view the pivot table.

Here's how the pivot table should look after Excel finishes its work:

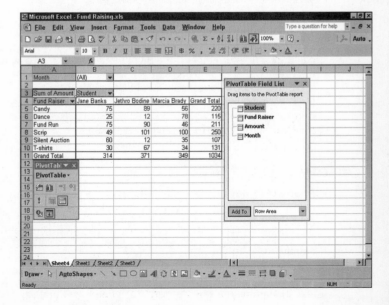

You can change how Excel summarizes the pivot table's information by dragging the field buttons to different locations in the table. For example, if you'd rather see each student's fund-raising activities summarized by month, drag the fields around so that the table appears as shown in the figure:

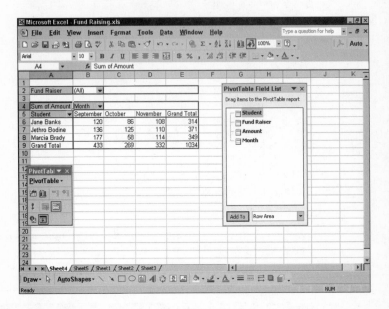

 The PivotTable Field List is a new feature for Excel designed to make it easier to rearrange the fields that make up the Pivot Table. You can drag a field directly off the PivotTable Field List into an area of the Pivot Table. Or you can select a field, use the drop-down list at the bottom of the PivotTable Field List to select the Pivot Table area that you want to move the field to, and then click the Add To button. To remove a field from the PivotTable, drag the field from the Pivot Table back to the PivotTable Field List.

Printing a Worksheet

Printing in Excel is pretty much the same as printing in any other Office 2000 application: You can choose File⇨Print, press Ctrl+P, or click the Print button in the Standard toolbar to print the current worksheet. Excel, however, offers a few printing tricks that you should know about:

✔ By default, Excel prints the entire worksheet. However, you can set a print area to print just part of the worksheet. First, highlight the range you want to print. Then choose File⇨Print Area⇨Set Print Area. A box with a dashed border will appear around the area you selected so that you can see the portion of your worksheet that will be printed.

✔ To clear the print area so that the entire worksheet prints, choose File⇨Print Area⇨Clear Print Area.

✔ If annoying grid lines appear on your printed output, choose File⇨Page Setup to call up the Page Setup dialog box. Click the Sheet tab and then click Gridlines to remove the check mark. Click OK to dismiss the Page Setup dialog box.

✔ To add a header or footer that appears at the top or bottom of every page, call up File⇨Page Setup and click the Header/Footer tab. Then type the header or footer in the appropriate text box and click OK.

Referencing Spreadsheet Cells

Excel uses a special type of notation to refer to cells within a worksheet. Each column in a worksheet is assigned a letter — A, B, C, and so on. Columns beyond column Z use two letters, so the columns that come after column Z are columns AA, AB, AC, and so on. Rows are numbered, starting with 1.

Each cell is given an *address* that is a combination of its column letter and row number. Thus the cell at the intersection of column E and row 5 is cell E5.

A *range* of cells is a rectangular area that is identified by two cells at opposite corners, separated by a colon. Thus the range C7:E10 is all the cells in a rectangle with its upper-left corner at cell C7 and lower-right corner at E10.

Sometimes you may see cell addresses that use dollar signs ($), such as D$9, $E7, or H22. The dollar sign designates the row or column portion of an address as *absolute*, meaning that Excel shouldn't try to adjust the address if you move or copy a formula that includes the absolute address. For example, suppose that you type the formula **=D3+D4** into cell D5 and then copy cell D5 to cell E5; Excel adjusts the formula to =E3+E4. But if you make the formula in cell D5 **=$D3+$D4**, Excel does *not* adjust the formula if you copy cell D5 to cell E5.

Here's a trick you can use with Excel: This program can use labels that appear above a column of numbers as cell addresses. For example, suppose that you set up a spreadsheet as shown in the figure:

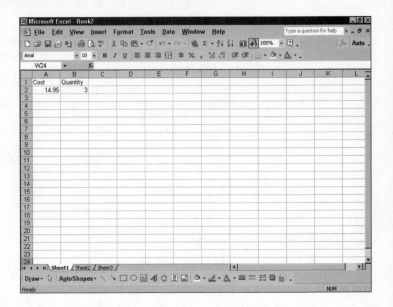

To create a formula in cell C2 that multiplies cells A2 and B2, you can enter =A2*B2. With Excel, however, you can enter the formula as =Cost*Quantity. Excel uses the column headings in row 1 to figure out that *Cost* is cell A2 and *Quantity* is cell B2.

Note that for this feature work, you must first call up the Tools⇨Options command, click the Calculations tab, then check the Accept Labels in Formulas option.

If your workbook has more than one worksheet, you can add the name of the sheet to the beginning of the cell reference, using an exclamation mark to separate the sheet name from the cell reference. For example, **Sheet1!A1** refers to cell A1 in the worksheet named Sheet1, and **Sheet4!B5:B10** refers to the range of cells from B5 through B10 in the worksheet named Sheet4.

You can also create a three-dimensional range of cells by specifying a range of sheets. For example, **Sheet1:Sheet4!D10** refers to cell D10 in all of the worksheets from Sheet1 to Sheet4.

Speech

One of the new features of Office is speech recognition, which allows you to dictate text into Office programs or speak voice commands. Excel has an additional speech feature that isn't found in the other Office programs: The ability to read your spreadsheet data out loud using a synthesized computer voice. You can have Excel read you an entire spreadsheet or a range of cells. And you can set up Excel so that it reads the contents of each cell aloud as you enter the data, which can help you confirm that you have entered the information correctly.

To activate the text-to-speech feature, choose the Tools⇨Speech⇨ Show Text to Speech Toolbar command. The Text to Speech Toolbar appears, as shown in the figure:

You can use the Text to Speech feature by clicking the various buttons on the Text to Speech Toolbar:

 ✔ **Speak Cells:** Begins speaking the contents of the selected cells. If you don't select a range of cells first, Excel recites the contents of the current cell plus any adjacent cells that are not empty.

 ✔ **Stop Speaking:** Tells Excel to shut up. This is handy if you start Excel on a long speech and get bored.

 ✔ **By Rows:** Tells Excel to read cells one row at a time. Each cell in the first row of the selection is read, then the cells in the second row are read, and so on.

 ✔ **By Columns:** Tells Excel to read cells one column at a time. Each cell in the first column of the selection is read, then the cells in the second column are read, and so on.

 ✔ **Speak on Enter:** Tells Excel to read the contents of each cell when you press Enter, Tab, one of the arrow keys. This is especially useful when you are entering data. When Excel reads the cell value aloud, you can verify that you entered the data correctly.

For details about using dictation or speech commands in Excel and other Office programs, see Part I.

Styles

Excel gives you the option of applying styles to your worksheet (or to portions of your worksheet) to create a unified and professional-looking design. Unlike AutoFormat, the Styles feature allows you to select from a limited choice of previously designed styles, or you can design your own.

Applying a style

To apply a style to your worksheet:

1. Highlight the cell or cells that you want to format with a particular style.

2. Select Format⇨Style. The Style dialog box opens, as shown here:

3. Click the Style Name drop-down list to see your style choices. Choose one that works for you.

4. Click OK, and your designated cells are formatted with the appropriate style.

Creating a style

To create a new style for your worksheets:

1. Apply whatever formatting you want to use to a cell or range of cells.

2. Highlight the cell or range of cells that you want to base the new style on.

3. Select Format⇨Style.

4. In the Style Name drop-down list, type a name for your style.

5. In the Style Includes section of the dialog box, click those features that you want included in the new style.

6. Click the Modify button. The Format Cells dialog box opens.

7. Move through the six tabs of this dialog box and determine what features you want in your new style.

8. Click OK to return to the Style dialog box. The dialog box now shows the features of your new style, as shown in the figure:

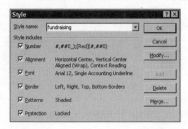

9. Click OK and look at the new style on your spreadsheet.

Unfortunately, you can only use this style in the spreadsheet where you created it. If you want to use it in a different spreadsheet, you can either re-create it from scratch, or you can use the Format Painter to copy the style in its original document and copy it to the new spreadsheet.

To delete a style, call up the Format⇨Style dialog box, select the style you want to delete from the drop-down list, and press the Delete key.

Web Queries

A *Web Query* is a way to include data from an Internet Web page in an Excel spreadsheet so that the data is kept up to date. Although Web Queries have been around for several versions of Excel, Excel is the first version that allows you to create Web Queries simply by copying and pasting data from a Web page to an Excel spreadsheet.

To create a Web query, follow these steps:

1. In your Web browser, find a page that contains information that you want to include in a spreadsheet. For example, the figure shows a page at MSN.com that includes stock quotes.

2. Drag the mouse over the information that you want to copy. Then right-click the selection and choose Copy from the pop-up menu that appears.

3. Fire up Excel and open the spreadsheet that you want to insert the Web data into. (If Excel is already running, press Alt+Tab to switch to Excel.)

4. Click the cell where you want to insert the Web data and then choose Edit⇨Paste.

5. When the pasted data appears, click the Paste Options icon (shown in the margin) that appears near the lower-right corner of the pasted data. This reveals a pop-up menu, as shown in the figure:

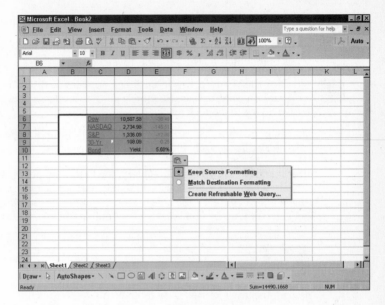

6. Choose Create Refreshable Web Query from the pop-up menu. This calls up the New Web Query dialog box, shown here:

The New Web Query dialog box shows a preview of the Web page that the data was copied from. In addition, every table of information on the page that can be used in a Web query is highlighted by the yellow arrow icon shown in the margin.

7. Click the yellow arrow icon, which appears next to the data that you want to base the query on. The icon changes from an arrow to a check mark.

8. Click the Import button (located at the bottom of the New Web Query dialog box).

After you have set up the Web Query, the External Data toolbar appears whenever you click a cell that is part of the query, as shown in the figure. (If the External Data toolbar doesn't appear, you can call it up by choosing View⇨Toolbars⇨External Data.)

You can use the External Data toolbar to refresh the contents of the Web Query or to change how often the contents are automatically refreshed. The following paragraphs describe the functions of the buttons on the External Data toolbar:

✔ **Edit Query:** Enables you to change the Web data used for the query.

✔ **Data Range Properties:** Lets you change several options for the query, including automatic updates and formatting information.

✔ **Refresh Data:** Obtains updated data for the query.

✔ **Cancel Refresh:** Cancels a refresh in progress.

✔ **Refresh All:** Refreshes all queries in the worksheet.

✔ **Refresh Status:** Displays information about the progress of a refresh.

PowerPoint 2002

If you like to stand in front of a group of people with a flip chart and a pointer, either trying to get them to buy something from you or convincing them to vote for you, then you'll love PowerPoint. PowerPoint creates presentations that can be printed out on plain paper, made into transparencies or 35mm slides, or shown on-screen or with a projector as an online presentation.

This part shows how to perform the most common PowerPoint chores. For more complete information about using PowerPoint, get a copy of my book, *PowerPoint 2002 For Windows For Dummies*, published by Hungry Minds, Inc.

In this part . . .

Animation Schemes

PowerPoint offers many new features for animating your slides. The easiest way to apply animation is to use the built-in animation schemes, which enable you to set the slide transitions and animation effects for title and bullet lists with just a few mouse clicks. You can set a different animation scheme for each slide in your presentation, or you can apply a single animation scheme to the entire presentation for a more consistent look.

You can work with animation schemes in Normal view or Slide Sorter view. Here are the steps:

1. If you are working in Normal view, call up the slide that you want to apply the animation scheme to. If you are in Slide Sorter view, click the slide that you want to animate. (You can skip this step if you want to apply an animation scheme to all of the slides in a presentation.)

You can change to Normal or Slide Sorter view by clicking the appropriate View button near the bottom-left corner of the PowerPoint window or by choosing the View➪Normal or View➪Slide Sorter command.

2. Choose Slide Show➪Animation schemes. The Slide Design pane appears at the right side of the window, as shown in the figure.

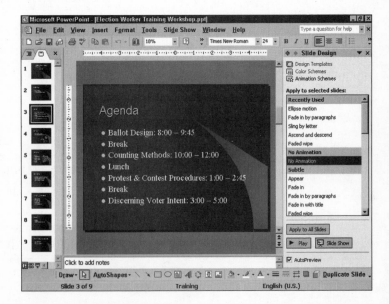

If the Task pane is already visible at the right side of the window, you can choose Slide Design⇨Animation Schemes from the drop-down menu at the top of the Task pane.

3. Click the animation scheme that you want to use from the scrollable list that appears. PowerPoint automatically animates the slide for you so you can preview how the animation effect looks. To see the animation again, click the Play button that appears near the bottom of the Slide Design pane.

The animation schemes listed in the Slide Design pane are organized into categories: No Animation, Subtle, Moderate, and Exciting. For your convenience, PowerPoint lists the five animation schemes that you've used most recently at the top of the list.

If you don't like the animation scheme that you selected, click another one. Each time you click on an animation scheme, PowerPoint applies the scheme to the current slide and displays a preview of the animation.

To remove all animation from the slide, choose the No Animation scheme.

4. To apply an animation to all of the slides in your presentation, click the Apply to All Slides button that appears near the bottom of the Slide Design pane.

To view your clever animations, click the Slide Show button in the lower-left corner of the screen, or choose the View⇨Slide Show command or press F5.

You can also apply an animation scheme to the Slide Master to apply consistent animations throughout your presentation. For more information, see "Slide Masters" later in this part.

AutoContent Wizard

If you're not sure how to get started on a presentation, you can use the AutoContent Wizard to create a skeleton presentation, which you can then modify by filling in the details. Here's the procedure:

1. If the New Presentation pane is not already visible, choose File⇨New command.

2. Click From the AutoContent Wizard in the New section of the New Presentation pane. The AutoContent Wizard comes to life:

3. Click the Next button. AutoContent Wizard asks you what type of presentation do you want to create. To see a full list of the options, click the All button.

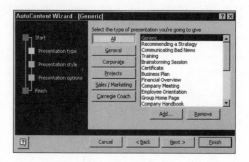

4. Select the presentation that you want to create from the list box that appears, and then click the Next button. The wizard asks what kind of output you want to create for the presentation. This depends on how the presentation will be used. You have several choices, depending on whether it's a live presentation (on-screen presentation, black and white overheads, color overheads, or 35mm slides) or an online presentation (called a *Web presentation*).

5. Select the type of presentation that you want to use and then click the Next button.

6. Select the output options that you want and then click the Next button. The wizard asks for the presentation title and what elements to include on each slide, including a footer, the date you updated your presentation, and whether you want your slides numbered. You can leave these fields blank if you don't want to bother with them.

7. Type the requested information in the appropriate fields and then click the Next button. The wizard displays its final screen.

8. Click the Finish button to create the presentation.

Clip Art

You can add clip art to your presentation by using the Insert⇨ Picture⇨Clip Art command. This command brings up the Insert Clip Art task pane, from which you can search for clip art from the various sources, including Microsoft's only clip art library. *See also* Part VII.

Several of PowerPoint's slide layouts include placeholders for clip art objects. To add clip art using one of these slide layouts, follow these steps:

1. Select the slide that you want to add clip art to.

2. Choose the Format⇨Slide Layout command to call up the Slide Layout pane.

If the task pane is already visible, you can call up the Slide Layout pane by choosing Slide Layout from the drop-down menu at the top of the task pane.

3. Choose one of the layouts that includes a Clip Art placeholder or a Content placeholder. Look for layouts that include the clip art icon shown in the margin. If this icon is in a placeholder by

itself, the slide will include a Clip Art placeholder. If the icon appears with other icons that represent a chart, diagram, video, and so on, the slide will include a Content placeholder.

The figure shows a slide that uses the Text & Clip Art layout.

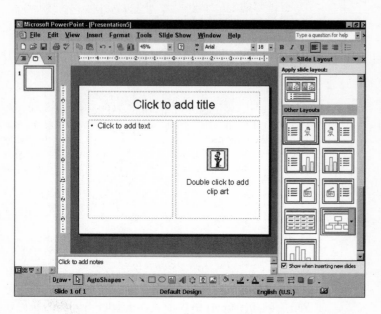

 4. If the slide layout includes a Clip Art placeholder, double-click the placeholder. If the slide has a Content placeholder instead, click the small Clip Art button (shown in the margin) located in the upper right-hand corner of the placeholder. Either way, the Select Picture dialog box appears, as shown in the figure.

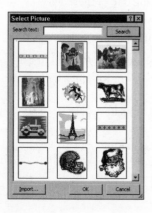

5. In the Search Text box, type a word or phrase that describes the picture you want to find, and then click the Search button. Pictures that meet your description appear in the Select Picture dialog box.

6. Click the picture that you want to use and then click OK. The picture is inserted, as shown in the figure.

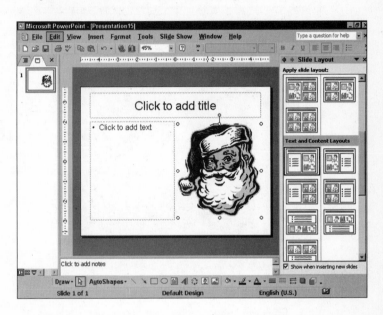

 For more information, see Chapter 11 of *PowerPoint For Windows For Dummies*.

Color Schemes

A *color scheme* is a set of coordinated colors that are used for various elements of your slides, such as the slide background, title text, body text, and so on. You can easily change the color scheme for a slide or the entire presentation by following this procedure:

1. Go to a slide to change its color scheme. (If you want to change the color scheme for all slides in a presentation, you can skip this step.)

2. Choose Format⇨Slide Design to call up the Slide Design pane; then click the Color Schemes link at the top of the Slide Design pane.

> **TIP**
> If the task pane is already visible, you can choose Slide Design from the drop-down menu at the top of the task pane to bring up the Slide Design pane.

The figure shows the Color Schemes options on the Slide Design pane.

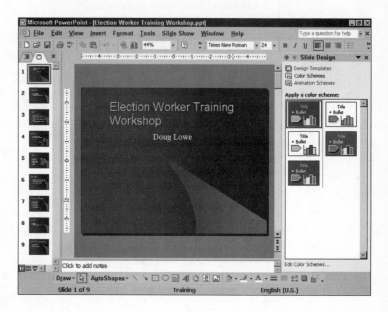

3. Click the color scheme that you want to use.

4. If you want to change the color scheme of all the slides in your presentation, click the down arrow next to the color scheme that you want to use, and then choose Apply to All Slides from the menu that appears.

To customize the color scheme, click the Edit Color Schemes link that appears at the bottom of the Slide Design pane to bring up the Edit Color Scheme dialog box, shown in the figure. Click the color scheme that you want to customize; then click the Custom tab at the top of the dialog box. Then select a slide element (for example, Background or Text and Lines) and use the Change Color button to change the element's color. If you want your changes to be saved as a new color scheme, click the Add as Standard Scheme button. (Note that the Add as Standard Scheme button will be grayed out until you change at least one of the scheme's colors.)

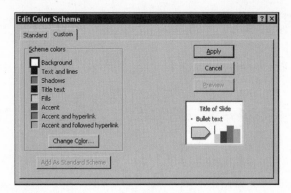

To change the color scheme for an entire presentation (including new slides you may create later), switch to Slide Master view by choosing View⇨Master⇨Slide Master.

Custom Animations

Animation allows you to add movement to your slides, which can help keep your audience awake. Every object on a slide can have its own animation effect. You can control the order in which objects are animated, the type of effect for each animation, and whether animations are manually controlled or happen automatically after a certain time has passed. To add animation to your presentation, follow these steps:

1. Make sure that you are in Normal view and scroll to the slide you want to animate.

2. Choose Slide Show⇨Custom Animation. The Custom Animation pane appears to the right of the slide.

If the Task pane is already visible, you can call up the Custom Animation pane by choosing Custom Animation from the drop-down list at the top of the Task pane.

3. Select an object on your slide that you want to animate by clicking the object.

4. Click Add Effect; then choose Entrance from the menu that appears. Choose the type of animation you want for the object from the menu. If you don't like any of the effects that appear in the Add Effect⇨Entrance menu, choose More Effects to call up the Add Entrance Effect dialog box, shown in the figure. Then choose the effect that you want to use and click OK.

When you choose an animation effect, PowerPoint animates the slide for you so that you can see how the animation looks. The figure shows a slide after a Fly In effect has been applied to the body text.

Notice the numbers to the left of the body text placeholder. PowerPoint displays a number next to each animated object or paragraph. A corresponding number appears in the list of animations in the Custom Animation pane so that you can see which animation effect has been applied to each slide object.

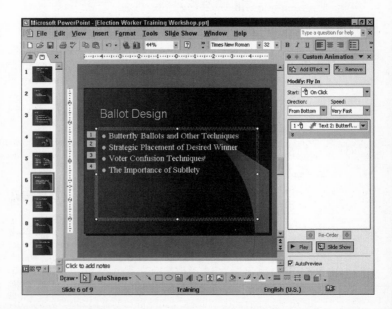

5. Play with the other controls on the Custom Animation pane to further tweak your custom animation. You can set the speed of the animation, and for many of the effects, you can also set the direction.

6. Repeat Steps 2 through 5 for any other objects that you want to animate.

For more control over an animation, click the down arrow to the right of the animation in the Custom Animation pane, then choose Effect Options from the menu that appears. Doing so calls up the Effect Options dialog box, shown in the figure. From this dialog box, you can change the animation direction, add sound to the animation, or change the object's color when the animation finishes. You can also click the Timing tab to change the speed of the animation and to start the animation automatically. From the Text Animation tab, you can also specify how paragraphs in a list should be animated.

To animate the paragraphs of a text object separately, call up the Effect Options dialog box and click the Text Animation tab, as shown in the figure. From the Group Text drop-down box, choose By First Level Paragraphs, and then check In Reverse Order if you want the paragraphs to appear in reverse order, starting with the one at the bottom of the order.

You can also add slide transition effects that are applied as each slide is displayed. *See also* "Transitions."

Inserting Slides from Other Presentations

You can use the Insert⇨Slides command from the Files menu to copy files from another presentation into the presentation that you're working on. Here are the steps:

1. In Normal or Slide Sorter view, move to the location where you want to insert a slide copied from another presentation.

2. Choose Insert⇨Slides from Files. The following box appears.

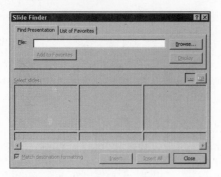

3. Click the Browse button to call up the Browse dialog box, shown in the figure:

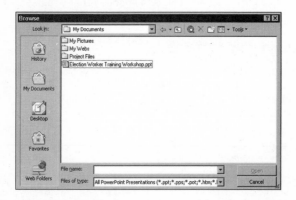

4. Locate the file that you want to copy slides from and click the Open button to return to the Slide Finder dialog box. The slides in the presentation are displayed as shown in the figure.

If the slides don't display, click the Display button.

5. Select the slides that you want to insert.

6. Click the Insert button to insert the slides into your presentation. To select more than one slide, hold down Ctrl while clicking the slides that you want to select. You can also select a range of slides by clicking the first slide in the range, and then holding down Shift and clicking the last slide in the range. The two slides that you clicked plus any slides that appear between them are selected.

To insert all of the slides from the presentation, click the Insert All button.

7. Repeat Steps 5 and 6 to insert additional slides from the same presentation, or repeat Steps 3 through 6 to insert slides from another presentation.

8. When you have inserted all the slides that you need, click the Close button.

If you frequently insert slides from a particular presentation, you can add that presentation to your list of favorites so that you can access it quickly. Click Add to Favorites to add a presentation to the list of favorites. To copy slides from one of your favorite presentations, click the List of Favorites tab, then double-click the presentation that you want to copy slides from.

Keyboard Shortcuts

The following tables list the most useful keyboard shortcuts in PowerPoint. These are shortcuts that are specific to PowerPoint. You can find other keyboard shortcuts that work in all Office programs in the "Toolbar Table" in The Big Picture section of this book.

Keyboard shortcuts for editing slides

Shortcut	What It Does
Ctrl+Delete	Deletes from the insertion point to the end of the word.
Ctrl+Backspace	Deletes from the insertion point to the beginning of the word.
Ctrl+M	Inserts a new slide and calls up the Slide Layout pane.
Ctrl+Shift+M	Inserts a new slide but doesn't summon the Slide Layout pane.
Alt+Shift+D	Calls up the Header and Footer dialog box so you can insert the date on the Slide Master.

cont.

Shortcut	What It Does
Alt+Shift+T	Calls up the Header and Footer dialog box, so you can insert the time on the Slide Master.
Alt+Shift+P	Calls up the Header and Footer dialog box, so you can insert the slide number on the Slide Master.
Ctrl+D	Duplicates the selected objects.
Ctrl+(left arrow)	Moves the insertion point one word to the left.
Ctrl+(right arrow)	Moves the insertion point one word to the right.
Ctrl+(up arrow)	Moves the insertion point to the preceding paragraph. In the Slides or Outline pane, moves to the previous slide.
Ctrl+_	Moves the insertion point to the next paragraph. In the Slides or Outline pane, moves to the next slide.
Ctrl+End	Moves the insertion point to the end of the text in the current text object.
Ctrl+Home	Moves the insertion point to the beginning of the text in the current text object.

Keyboard shortcuts for formatting text

Shortcut	What It Does
Ctrl+Shift+F	Activates the font control in the Formatting toolbar, so you can change the font.
Ctrl+Shift+P	Activates the font size control on the Formatting toolbar, so you can change the point size.
Ctrl+Shift+>	Increases the point size to the next available size.
Ctrl+Shift+<	Decreases the point size to the preceding size.
Ctrl+L	Left-aligns the paragraph.
Ctrl+R	Right-aligns the paragraph.
Ctrl+J	Justifies the paragraph.
Ctrl+E	Centers the paragraph.

Keyboard shortcuts for working with outlines

Shortcut	*What It Does*
Tab	Demotes the selected paragraphs.
Shift+Tab	Promotes the selected paragraphs.
Alt+Shift+ (up arrow)	Moves the selected paragraphs up.
Alt+Shift+ (down arrow)	Moves the selected paragraphs down.
Alt+Shift+A	Shows all text and headings.
Alt+Shift+-	Collapses all text under a heading.
Alt+Shift++	Expands all text under a heading.

Notes

PowerPoint enables you to create separate notes to accompany your slides to help you remember what you want to say. The beauty of notes is that the audience doesn't see them, so they think you're winging it.

You can print pages of notes that include a small image of the complete slide along with the notes for that slide. And, a new feature in PowerPoint enables you to display your notes on one monitor, while displaying your slides on a second monitor (or a projector) if your computer is equipped with two video ports. *See also* "Slide Show."

To add notes to a slide, follow this procedure:

1. In Normal view, find the slide that you want to add notes to.

2. Click in the Click to Add Notes window near the bottom of your screen.

3. Add the text of your notes in this window.

4. To see your Notes page, select View⇨Notes Page. This switches you to Notes view, as shown in the figure.

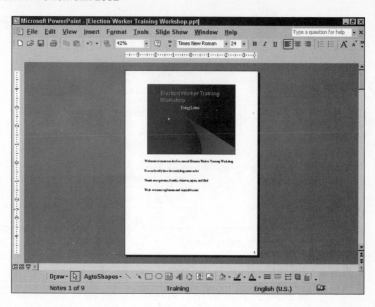

5. Adjust the zoom factor with the Zoom drop-down list on the Standard toolbar, if necessary, so you can read the text of your notes.

6. If necessary, scroll the display to bring the text into view. (The text of your notes appears beneath the slide image.)

7. If you want to add more text, click in the notes area and type to your heart's content.

The text that you type appears in the notes area. You can use any of the PowerPoint standard word processing features, such as cut, copy, and paste, while you create your notes. Press Enter to create new paragraphs.

 After you switch to Notes Page view, you don't have to return to Normal view to add notes for other slides. Use the scroll bar or PgUp and PgDn to add notes for other slides.

 To print Notes pages, choose the File⇔Print command to call up the Print dialog box. In the Print What drop-down box (located about two-thirds of the way down on the left side), choose Notes Pages, set any other print options that you want, and then click OK to print the Notes pages.

For more information, see Chapter 18 of *PowerPoint For Windows For Dummies.*

Photo Album

If you have a stack of photographs that you'd like to turn into a slide show and if you have a scanner attached to your computer, then you'll love the new Photo Album feature of PowerPoint. This feature can automatically create presentations that show off your pictures by arranging the pictures one, two, or four on a slide. And you can use special Photo Album templates to give your photo albums a jazzy look.

Although you can scan your pictures directly into PowerPoint, I prefer to scan the pictures separately, place them all in a single folder, and then fire up PowerPoint and create my photo album. Therefore, the following procedure assumes that you have already scanned your pictures and saved them in a folder:

1. In PowerPoint, close any open presentations.

2. Choose the Insert⇨Picture⇨New Photo Album. (If New Photo Album doesn't appear on the menu, click the down arrow located at the bottom of the menu.) The Photo Album dialog box appears, as shown in the figure.

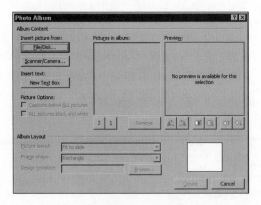

3. Click the File/Disk button (located near the top left of the Photo Album dialog box). Doing so calls up the Insert New Pictures dialog box, as shown in the figure.

4. Use the Look In drop-down box at the top of the Insert New Pictures dialog box to locate the folder that contains your pictures.

5. Select the pictures that you want to include in your photo album. You can select more than one picture by holding down Ctrl while clicking the pictures that you want to select. Or you can select a group of pictures by clicking the first picture in the group, holding down Shift, and clicking the last picture in the group. The two pictures that you clicked, plus any pictures listed between them, are selected.

TIP

If you want to include all of the pictures in the folder, click any of the pictures listed and then press Ctrl+A.

6. Click Insert. You are returned to the Photo Album dialog box, with the pictures that you selected listed in the Pictures in Album list as the figure shows.

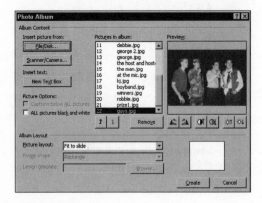

7. Use the up and down arrow buttons located below the Pictures In Album list to rearrange the order of your pictures.

8. Use the Picture Layout drop-down box to indicate how you want the pictures arranged on slides in your photo album presentation. The choices are Fit to Slide, 1 Picture, 2 Pictures, 4 Pictures, 1 Picture with Title, 2 Pictures with Title, and 4 Pictures with Title.

9. If you select any option other than Fit to Slide in Step 8, use the Frame Shape drop-down box to choose the shape of your picture frames (Rectangle, Rounded Rectangle, Beveled, and so on). Then click the Browse button to choose a template for your photo album. (The Browse button calls up a Choose Design Template dialog box. Click the Photo Album Templates folder, then double-click the template that you want to use.)

10. Click the Create button, located near the bottom of the Photo Album dialog box. PowerPoint creates a new presentation containing the pictures that you selected, as shown in the figure.

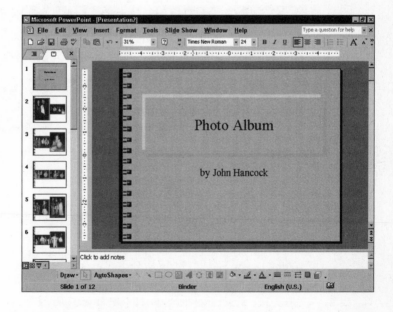

11. Change the title and subtitle on the title slide, and work your way through the presentation one slide at a time, adjusting the picture sizes and adding titles or any other elements that you want to add to each slide.

12. Choose File⇨Save to save your presentation.

Rearranging Slides

You can quickly rearrange slides by switching to Slide Sorter view, in which you can see a thumbnail version of each slide in a presentation. Here's the procedure:

1. Switch to Slide Sorter view by clicking the Slide Sorter view button at the bottom-left corner of the screen or by choosing View⇨Slide Sorter. PowerPoint switches to Slide Sorter view, as the figure shows:

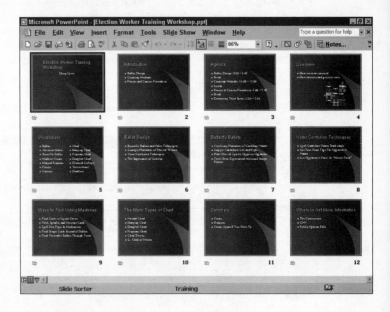

2. To move a slide, click and drag it to a new location. PowerPoint adjusts the display to show the new arrangement of slides and automatically renumbers the slides.

3. To delete a slide, click the slide and press Delete or choose Edit⇨Delete Slide. (Delete works on an entire slide only in Slide Sorter view.)

4. To add a new slide, click the slide that you want the new slide to follow and then click the New Slide button. A new slide is inserted and the Slide Layout pane appears. Click the slide layout that you want to use. To edit the contents of the slide, return to Normal view. (Unfortunately, the placeholders that are added to the slide when you choose the slide layout don't appear in Slide Sorter view. No matter which layout you apply to the new slide, the slide looks blank in Slide Layout view. After you switch to Normal view, however, you can see the placeholders.)

If your presentation contains more slides than can fit on-screen at the same time, you can use the scroll bars to scroll the display. Or you can change the zoom factor to make the slides smaller. Click the down arrow next to the zoom size and select a smaller zoom percentage.

Slide Layout

The Slide Layout governs the positions of the various objects on a slide. Each slide in a presentation can have a different layout. PowerPoint comes with 23 pre-designed layouts containing various combinations of placeholders for text objects, graphics, and other types of content. Here are the steps for applying one of these layouts to a slide:

1. In Normal view, go to a slide to change its layout.

2. Click the Format⇨Slide Layout command. The Slide Layout pane appears at the right of the PowerPoint window, as shown in the figure:

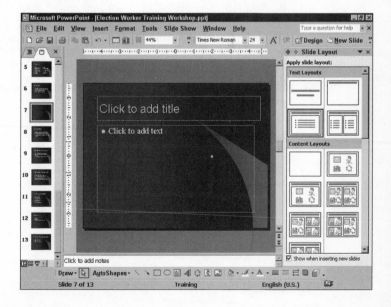

3. In the Slide Layout pane, click the layout that you want to use.

After you have applied the layout that you want, you can move or resize the placeholder objects by dragging the placeholder's border.

Slide Master

A Slide Master controls the overall appearance of the slides in your presentation. Slide Masters control the following information:

✔ Background color, image, or fill effect

✔ Color scheme

✔ Font styles for titles, body text, and other text elements

✔ Placeholder positions

✔ Text or graphic objects that should appear on each slide, such as your name or company logo

In addition to the Slide Master, each presentation also has a Title Master. Normally, the Title Master is used for the first slide in the presentation and the Slide Master is used for all other slides.

The following sections describe the most common procedures for working with Slide Masters.

Editing a master

Any edits or format changes that you make to the Slide Master apply to every slide in your presentation that is based on that Slide Master. To edit a Slide Master, follow these steps:

1. Choose the View➪Master➪Slide Master command. PowerPoint switches to Slide Master view, as shown in the figure:

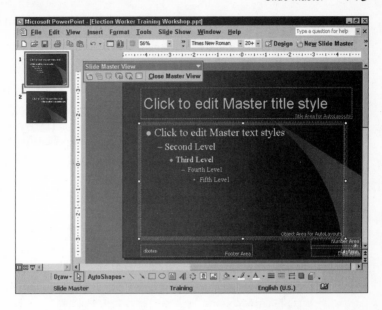

2. Edit the Slide Master however you want. Here are some suggestions:

   • To change the font style for a text paragraph, click the paragraph and use the Format⇨Font command or the font controls on the Formatting toolbar. (You don't have to select the entire paragraph; just click anywhere in the paragraph.)

   • To change the bullet style, click the paragraph level that you want to change, and then use the Format⇨Bullets and Numbering command to format the bullets however you want.

   • To change the background, use the Format⇨Background command. This command enables you to set the background to a specific color, use an image file for the background, or create a fill effect, such as a pattern or gradient fill.

   • To add a text object that you want to appear on every slide, use the Text Box tool located in the Drawing toolbar.

   • To add a shape that you want to appear on every slide, use the drawing controls on the Drawing toolbar to draw the shape directly onto the Slide Master.

3. When you are finished working on the master, click Close Master View in the floating Slide Master View toolbar.

The thumbnail slide images to the left of the Slide Master represent the Slide and Title Masters; the one on the top is the Slide Master, the one below it is the Title Master. To edit the Title Master, click the thumbnail Title Master slide.

Hiding background objects

Occasionally, you may want text or graphic objects that appear on the Slide Master to not appear on a particular slide. To do this, you must hide the background objects by following this procedure:

1. In Normal view, display the slide that you want to show with a plain background.

2. Choose Format⇨Background. The Background dialog box appears.

3. Check Omit Background Graphics from the Master check box.

4. Click the Apply button or press Enter.

This procedure for hiding background objects applies only to the current slide. Other slide pages are not affected. To hide background objects for all slides in your presentation, click the Apply to All button instead of the Apply button in Step 4.

Multiple masters

PowerPoint allows you to have more than one set of Slide and Title Masters in a single presentation. This feature makes it easier to create groups of slides with different formats within your presentation. The following buttons in the Slide Master View toolbar let you work with additional masters:

✔ Inserts a new Slide Master.

✔ Inserts a new Title Master.

✔ Deletes a Slide or Title Master.

✔ Changes the name of a Slide or Title Master.

If you have created more than one set of masters for a presentation, you can choose a master to use for a particular slide by selecting that slide in Slide Sorter or Normal view and choosing the Format⇨Slide Design. In the Slide Design pane, click the down arrow that appears next to the miniature image of the master that you want to use; then choose Apply to Selected Slides.

Slide Show

Your presentation is all prepared, the projector is set up, the audience has just arrived, and the emcee has just introduced you. Now it's time for the show. Here's the procedure for displaying your presentation:

1. Click the Slide Show View button to call up the first slide in your presentation.

   The handy mouse-free shortcut to start a slide show is F5.

2. To advance to the next slide, press Enter, press the spacebar, or click the left mouse button.

3. Press Esc to end the slide show.

During the slide show, you can use the following keyboard tricks:

To Do This	Press Any of These Keys
Display next slide	Enter, spacebar, right arrow, down arrow, PgDn, N
Display previous slide	Backspace, left arrow, up arrow, PgUp, P
Display first slide	1+Enter
Display specific slide	Slide number+Enter
Toggle screen black	B, period
Toggle screen white	W, (comma)
Show or hide pointer	A, = (equals)
Erase screen doodles	E
Stop or restart automatic show	S, + (plus)
Display next slide even if hidden	H
Display specific hidden slide	Slide number of hidden slide+Enter
Change pen to arrow	Ctrl+A
Change arrow to pen	Ctrl+P
End slide show	Esc, Ctrl+Break, - (minus)

To set up a presentation so that it runs continuously on the computer, choose Slide Show⇨Set Up Show to call up the Set Up Show dialog box. Check the "Loop Continuously until 'Esc' option" and the "Using Timings, if Present" option, and then click OK. Then click Slide Show⇨Rehearse Timings. This opens the slide show with a Timer dialog box that lets you manually set the timing for your slide show. As soon as it opens, the timer starts counting. Determine how long you want the slide to remain on the screen, and when you reach that time, click on the Next arrow. The screen moves to the next slide on the sequence and starts all over again. When you get to the end of the slides, a dialog box appears asking whether you want to use these timings. If you're happy with the timings, click Yes. The screen opens to Slide Sorter view, which allows you to see the times that you've set for each slide.

Summary Slides

You can quickly create a summary slide that contains the titles of some or all of the slides in your presentation by following these steps:

1. Switch to Slide Sorter view.

2. Select the slides that you want to include in the summary. To summarize the entire presentation, press Ctrl+A to select all the presentation's slides. If you want to base the summary on several slides that are not adjacent to one another (for example, using the first slide of each section of a presentation), hold down the Ctrl key and click each of the slides you want to use.

3. Click the Summary Slide button, which is located on the Slide Sorter toolbar. This toolbar appears at the top of the screen, beneath the Formatting toolbar. PowerPoint inserts the summary slide in front of the selected slides.

Templates

A *template* is a PowerPoint presentation that is used as a model to create other presentations. You can select a template when creating a presentation by choosing From Design Template in the New Presentation pane.

If at any time you decide that you don't like the appearance of your presentation, you can change the presentation's appearance without changing its contents by assigning a new template to the presentation. To do that, follow these steps:

1. Choose Format⇨Slide Design. The Slide Design pane appears, as shown in the figure.

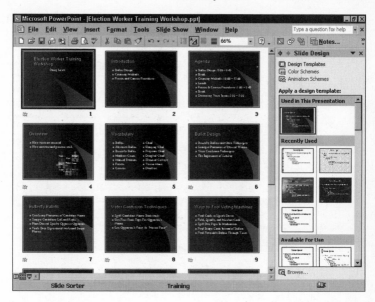

2. Click the template that you want to use.

TIP If you want to apply a template just to one slide or to only some of the slides in your presentation, switch to Slide Sorter view. Then select the slides that you want to apply the template to, click the down arrow on the right of the template that you want to use, and choose Apply to Selected Slides.

Transitions

A *transition* is a visual effect that appears when a PowerPoint slide show moves from one slide to the next. PowerPoint lets you choose from among many different transition effects, and you can specify a different effect for each slide. Additionally, you can easily add sound effects to plug even more pizzazz into your presentations. To set the transitions between slides, follow this procedure:

1. Switch to Normal view or Slide Sorter view by choosing View➪Normal or View➪Slide Sorter.

2. Select the slide that you want to add a transition. Note that the transition always occurs before the slide that you select. To set the transition to occur between the first and second slides, select the second slide.

3. Choose Slide Show➪Slide Transition. The Slide Transition pane appears, as shown in the figure.

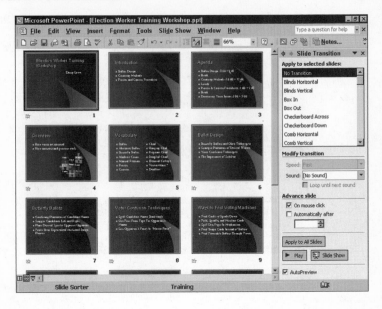

4. Select the transition effect that you want from the Effect drop-down list box.

5. Select the speed of the transition by setting the Speed drop-down control to Slow, Medium, or Fast.

6. If you want, choose a sound to accompany the transition from the Sound drop-down box.

7. If you want the slide show to run automatically, check the Automatically After check box and then enter the number of seconds that you want the slide displayed. If you want to control the pace of the slide show, check the On Mouse Click check box.

To apply the same transition effect to all of the slides in your presentation, set the transition effect, speed, and sound, and then click the Apply to All button located at the bottom of the Slide Transition pane.

Viewer

You can transfer a PowerPoint presentation to a disk, from which you can run the presentation on any computer enabled with Windows 95 or later, by using a special program called the PowerPoint Viewer. The following sections cover the procedures for using the Viewer.

Using the Pack and Go Wizard

To prepare a presentation for use with the PowerPoint Viewer, use the Pack and Go Wizard. Here's the procedure:

1. Open the presentation that you want to move to another computer.

2. Choose File⇨Pack and Go. The Pack and Go Wizard appears.

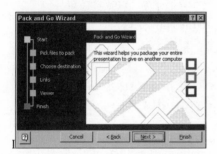

3. Click Next. The Wizard asks which presentation you want to include. You can choose between the presentation you have open (Active presentation), another presentation (Other presentation), or both. If you choose Other presentation, the Browse feature activates, which allows you to locate the other presentation on your system.

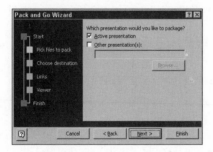

4. Click Next. The Wizard asks whether you want to copy the presentation to drive A or to a different drive or network location.

5. Change the destination if necessary and then click Next. The Wizard now asks whether you want to Include Linked Files and Embed TrueType fonts. It's usually a good idea to check both options.

6. Click Next again. The Wizard asks whether you want to include the PowerPoint Viewer. It's best to include the Viewer, just in case the computer that you want to run the presentation on doesn't have PowerPoint installed.

If the Viewer isn't installed on your computer, click Download the Viewer to download the Viewer from Microsoft's Web site, then follow the instructions that appear on the screen.

7. Click Next. The wizard's final screen appears.

8. Insert a disk into the hard drive.

9. Click the Finish button.

Copying a packed presentation onto another computer

You can't run a presentation directly from the disk that's created by the Pack and Go Wizard. Instead, you must first copy the presentation from the disk onto another computer's hard drive by following these steps:

1. Insert the disk that contains the packed presentation into the hard drive on the computer from which you want to run the presentation.

2. Open the My Computer window by double-clicking its icon and then select the hard drive into which you inserted the disk.

3. Double-click the Pngsetup icon to run the Pack and Go Setup program.

4. Follow the instructions that appear on-screen.

Running a slide show by using the Viewer

After you copy the presentation to the other computer, you can run it with the Viewer by following this procedure:

1. Start the PowerPoint Viewer by double-clicking its icon in the folder into which you copied the presentation. The system extracts the Viewer onto your hard drive, and the program asks whether you want to run the slide show at this time.

2. Click Yes. Your slide show starts automatically.

Unfortunately, the PowerPoint Viewer doesn't support most of the new animation features of PowerPoint. If you need to distribute your presentation using the Viewer, limit your animations to basic transitions and builds.

Access 2002

Access is the powerful database program that comes with Microsoft Office XP Professional. Because the Standard Edition of Office XP doesn't include Access, you can skip this part if you don't have Office XP Professional.

Although Access is a powerful database program that computer programmers use to create sophisticated applications, you don't need a Ph.D. in computer science to use Access. By using the information in this part, you can create simple databases, design custom forms and reports, and query your database to extract important information. For more information about Access, pick up a copy of *Access 2002 For Dummies,* by John Kaufeld, published by Hungry Minds, Inc.

In this part . . .

Database Wizard

Creating a database from scratch can be a tedious chore and is best left to database experts. Access, however, comes with a friendly Database Wizard that can perform most of the dirty work for you. All you need to do is answer a few simple questions and enjoy a cup of coffee while the Wizard creates your database fields, forms, and reports. Just follow these steps:

1. Click General Templates in the New From Template section of the New File pane to summon the Templates dialog box. If you already have another database open, close it by choosing File⇨Close, and then choose File⇨New, or simply click the New button to summon the New File pane. Then click General Templates in the New From Template section.

2. Click the Databases tab of the Templates dialog box to reveal the list of Database templates, as shown in the following figure:

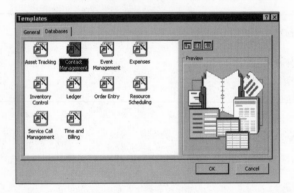

3. From the list of database templates, click the one that best represents the type of database that you want to create.

4. Click OK. The File New Database dialog box appears, as shown in the figure.

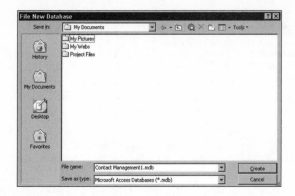

5. Use the Save In drop-down list box to locate the folder that you want to store your new database in. Then, type a name for your database in the File Name text box or leave the name that Access proposes if it's satisfactory.

6. Click the Create button. Access whirs and spins for a moment and then displays the first screen of the Database Wizard, as shown in the figure:

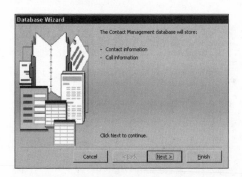

7. Click the Next button to start the wizard. The wizard proposes certain fields to be included in the database but allows you to select which ones should actually be included, as shown in the figure:

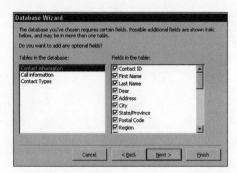

8. Scan the fields in the table list, adding or removing fields from the proposed list of fields for each table by clicking the check box next to the field name.

If the database has more than one table, select the table that you want to examine from the list of database tables.

9. After you're satisfied with the arrangement of fields for the table, click the <u>N</u>ext button. The wizard then asks what style you want to use for dialog boxes that are used by the database, as shown in the following figure:

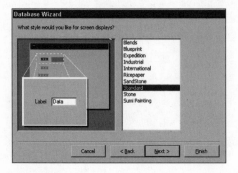

10. Select the display style that suits your fancy and then click the <u>N</u>ext button. The wizard now asks for your report style preference, which affects elements like the typeface and background colors for your reports, as shown in the figure:

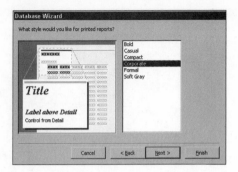

11. From the list, select the report style that pleases you and then click the Next button. The wizard asks a few more annoying questions, including what you want to name your database.

12. Type a title for the database in the text box if you aren't satisfied with the wizard's proposed title.

13. If you want to include a picture in all the reports for the database, check the Yes, I'd Like to Include a Picture check box; then click the Picture button and select a picture for the reports.

14. Click the Next button. The wizard displays its final screen, which displays a checkered flag as if to boast that creating a database in Access is as hard as winning at Daytona.

15. Click the Finish button. Be patient while the wizard creates the database tables, forms, and reports. After the wizard finishes, Access opens the database.

Notice that the Database Wizard creates a Switchboard, which serves as a customized menu for each type of database. To use the Switchboard, just click the buttons that appear next to each option.

To dismiss the Switchboard, click the Switchboard's Close button in the upper-right corner. Then you can open the minimized window for the database and use the Access database functions directly.

Entering Data

After you create a database, you can enter data into it. The exact procedures that you must follow vary depending on the database, but here's a general procedure you can use:

1. From the Main Switchboard for the database, select an option that allows you to enter data. For example, the figure shows the Main Switchboard for a Contact Management database. The first two items on this switchboard enable you to enter data.

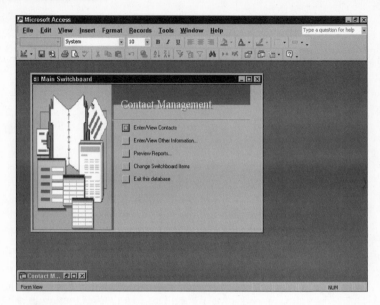

Selecting the first option on this switchboard brings up the following data entry form:

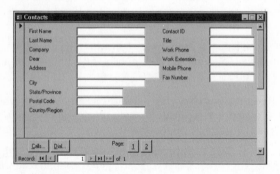

2. Type the information for each field, using the Tab key to move from field to field.

3. After you have entered all the information for one record, click the New Record button to create the record. You can then enter data for another record.

4. After you finish entering data, click the form's Close button (the X in the top-right corner) to dismiss the form.

You can change data in an existing record by using one of the navigation buttons that appear at the bottom of the form to display the record. Then, use the Tab key to move to the field that you want to change, type a new value into the field, and press Enter. The navigation buttons are described in the following table:

Navigation Button	What It Does
⏮	Displays the first record in the database.
◀	Goes back one record.
▶	Goes forward one record.
⏭	Displays the last record in the database.

To delete a record, use the navigation buttons to call up the record that you want to delete and then choose Edit⇨Delete Record. A dialog box appears, warning you that you are about to delete information and that it won't be retrievable. If you really want to delete the record, click the Yes button.

Fields

After you create a database, adding, deleting, or changing the properties of fields in your database tables is a simple matter. The following sections describe how.

Working in Table Design view

To add new fields or to change or delete existing fields in a table, you must first switch to the table's design view. Follow these steps:

1. If the database's Switchboard is open, close the window by clicking its Close button (located in the upper-right corner, marked by an X) and then open the minimized Database window, as shown in the figure. (The *Switchboard* is a menu that lets you access common database functions, such as entering data or printing reports. The databases that are created by the Access database templates all include Switchboards.)

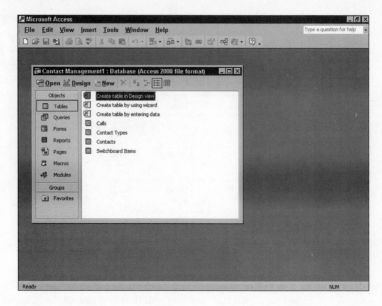

On the left side of the Database screen is an Objects list.

2. In the Objects list, click the Tables button to access the database tables. Then, click the table that you want to add a field to and click the Design button located at the top of the Tables window.

The first three items listed in the Tables window provide three different methods for creating new tables. Following these three items, you find your database tables listed. When you click the table that you want to add a field to, the Table window appears, as shown in the figure:

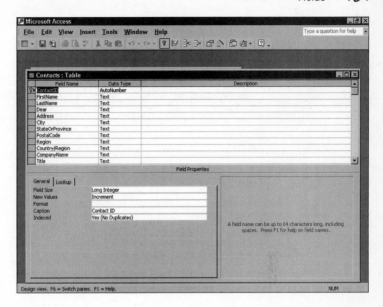

In Design view, you can work with the table's fields as described in the following procedures. After you're finished working with the table's design, click the Close button located in the upper-right corner of the table design window. When Access asks whether you want to save changes to the table design, click Yes to save your design changes.

Adding a field using the Field Builder

Access includes a tool called *Field Builder* that enables you to create new fields based on the fields in the sample databases that come with Access. Open the table in Design view, and then follow these steps:

1. Click the row in which you want to insert the new field. To insert the new field after the existing fields, click the first blank row.

 If you click an already-formatted field and follow these instructions, that already-formatted field is replaced by the new one that you chose. If you want to add a field without removing any of the old ones, you must first insert a field by clicking the Insert Rows button. Clicking this button inserts a new field immediately before the field that is currently highlighted.

 2. Click the Build button on the Standard toolbar. The Field Builder dialog box appears, as shown in the figure:

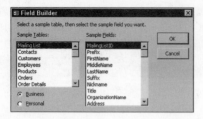

3. Select from the Sample Tables list the sample table that contains the field you want to add and then select the field from the Sample Fields list.

4. Click OK. Access adds the field to the table and closes the dialog box.

5. Click the Close button in the upper-right corner of the Table Design window.

6. Access asks whether you want to save changes to the table design. Click the Yes button.

Adding fields manually

If you prefer to define the field manually or if no similar field exists in any of the sample databases, call up the Table Design view. *See also* "Working in table design view." Then, follow these steps:

1. To insert the new field after the existing fields, click the first blank row.

   To insert the new field among the existing fields, click where you want to insert the new field and then click the Insert Row button on the toolbar.

2. Type the name of the new field in the Field Name column.

3. Click in the Data Type column of that field. An arrow appears on the right side of the column.

4. Click the arrow to see a drop-down list of field types.

5. Select the field type that you want to use for this field.

6. Adjust the properties for the field as necessary, using the properties list that appears at the bottom of the Table window. To change one of the property settings, click the property and type a new value.

Changing and deleting fields

To change the name, type, or properties of a field, click the field's row in the Table Design window, and then change any of the field settings that you want to. For example, to change the field name, click the field name and type a new name. To change the field type, change the Data Type setting. And to change the field's properties, change the property settings for the field, listed at the bottom of the Table Design window.

 To delete a field, click the field's row, then press the Delete key or click the Delete Rows button.

Form Wizard

One of the best features of Access is that the program enables you to create custom-designed forms for data that you create or retrieve from your database. You can spend hours creating forms from scratch, or you can create a basic form in minutes by using the Form Wizard. To use the wizard, just follow these steps:

1. Choose File⇨Open to open the database that you want to create a form for, click Forms in the object list, and then double-click Create Form by Using Wizard in the Forms window. The Form Wizard appears, as shown in the figure:

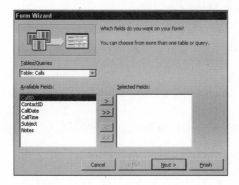

2. Select the fields that you want to include on the form. To select the fields, first select the table or query from the Tables/Queries list containing the field that you want to include on the form. In the Available Fields list, click the field that you want to include and then click the > button. Access removes the field that you select from the Available Fields list and inserts the field in the Selected Fields list. Repeat this step for each field that you want to include.

 You can move all the fields from the Available Fields list over to the Selected Fields list by clicking the >> button. And you can remove fields from the Selected Fields by clicking < (or << to remove them all). Fields you remove from the Selected Fields list are returned to the Available Fields list.

3. After you select all the fields that you want to include, click the Next button. The Form Wizard dialog box asks how you want the fields arranged on the form, as shown in the figure:

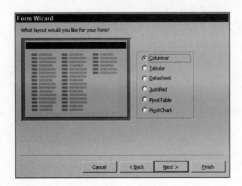

4. Select the radio button for the field layout that you want. You have the following choices of form layouts:

   • **Columnar:** Arranges fields in a column, with one record shown on each form.

   • **Tabular:** Arranges fields in a tabular form, with one row of fields for each record. This format displays more than one record at a time.

   • **Datasheet:** Arranges fields in a spreadsheet-like configuration. This layout also shows more than one record at a time.

   • **Justified:** Arranges fields in a grid configuration, adjusting the width of each field so that the table aligns on both the left and right sides. If possible, the Form Wizard places more than one field in each row of the grid. In this layout, only one record is visible at a time.

   • **Pivot Table:** Arranges fields as a pivot table.

   • **Pivot Chart:** Arranges fields as a pivot chart.

5. Click the Next button. The Form Wizard asks which form style you prefer. These styles provide different background images and text styles.

6. From the list, select the style that you prefer and then click the Next button. The Form Wizard displays its final screen, as shown in the figure:

7. Type a title for the form in the text box and then click the Finish button. The wizard creates and then displays the form, as shown in the figure:

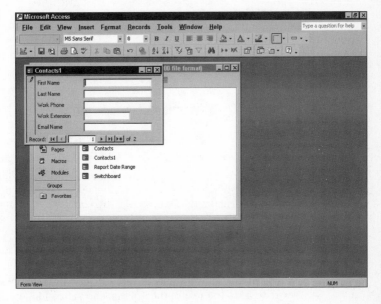

 For more information, see *Access 2002 For Dummies*.

Queries

A query is the most powerful and difficult-to-use feature of Access. Before you create a query, you need to know the following details:

- ✔ Which tables are involved in the query
- ✔ Which fields you want the query result to show

✔ Which sequence you want the query result sorted into

✔ Which criteria you want to apply to determine which records Access selects

Here's the blow-by-blow procedure for creating a query:

1. Open the database that you want to create a query for by choosing File⇨Open. Then click Queries in the Object list (on the left side of the Database window) and double-click Create Query in Design View. You are switched to Query Design view. When Query Design view first appears, a Query window in which you construct your query is partially overlaid by a Show Tables dialog box, which you use to select the table or tables to be used for the query, as shown in the figure.

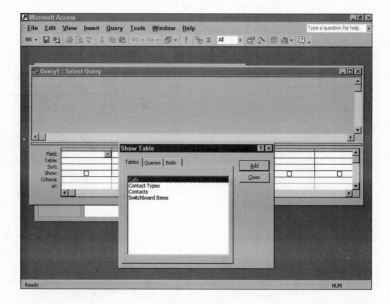

If you prefer, you can select Create a Query by Using Wizard. If you do, skip the rest of these steps and instead follow the instructions that the wizard offers.

2. Double-click each table that you want to include in the query. Each table that you add appears in its own little window floating in the upper portion of the Query window. After you have added all the tables that you want to use for the query, click the Close button to dismiss the Show Table dialog box.

TIP

Besides tables, you can also include other queries in a new query.

3. Double-click the fields in the tables (that you added to the Query window) that you want to include in the query. Each field that you select is added to a column in the bottom part of the Query window. The figure shows what the query window looks like after you select several fields:

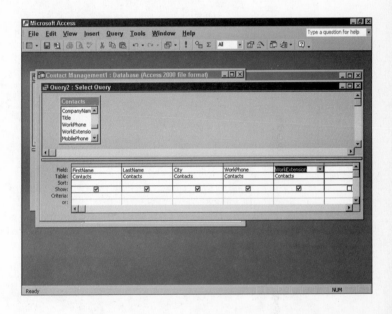

4. Select the sort order for the query result. You select the sort order by first clicking the sort row for each field that you want to sort the result by. Then, use the drop-down list box that appears to choose Ascending or Descending sequence. The figure shows a query that's sorted first by Last Name, and then by City.

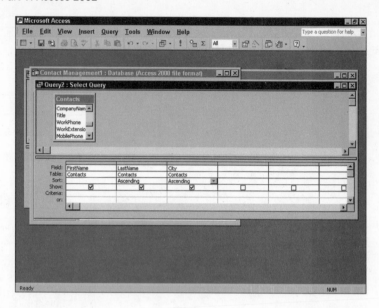

5. Type the query selection criteria in the Criteria rows of the fields with values that you want to test. In the example shown in the figure, the query tests the City field so that the result shows only those records in which the City field is "Pixley" or "Hooterville."

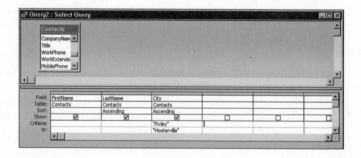

In the Criteria row you can use any of the symbols shown in the following table for more precise control over which records the query selects.

Symbol	Meaning
=	Equal to
<	Less than

Symbol	Meaning
>	Greater than
<=	Less than or equal to
>=	Greater than or equal to
<>	Not equal to

You can also specify a range of values by typing **Between...and**, as in **Between 10 and 50**. Or, you can type **Like** if you're not sure of the spelling.

6. Click the Run button on the toolbar to run the query. The query results appear in a separate window, as shown in the figure:

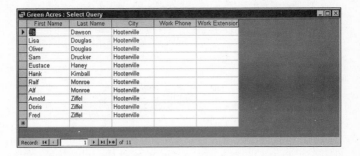

7. If the query doesn't work as you expect, close the query result by clicking the Close button in the upper-right corner of the Query Result window, and then work on the query settings to correct the problem. If the query does work as you expect, choose File⇨Save from the main menu to save the query. When the Save As dialog box appears, type a name for your query, then click OK.

After you save a query, you can run that query at any time by opening the Database window, clicking Queries in the Objects list, and then double-clicking the query name in the list of queries.

For more information, see Chapter 11 of *Access 2002 For Dummies*.

Reports

Creating a report in Access is easy if you use the Report Wizards. Report Wizards create various types of reports after asking you questions about the information that you want to include. The following procedure shows you how to create a simple report listing the database records from a single table, with one record per line and the fields neatly lined up in one column. The procedure for creating other types of reports is similar.

Here's the procedure for creating a report:

1. Choose File➪Open to open the database that you want to create a report for, click the Reports button in the Objects list on the left side of the Database window, and then double-click Create Report by Using Wizard. The Report Wizard appears, as shown in the figure:

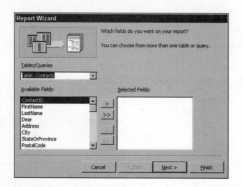

2. Select the fields that you want to include in the report. To select fields for the report, select the table that contains the fields that you want from the Tables/Queries drop-down list. Then in the Available Fields list, click the field that you want to include and click the > button. Access removes the field that you select from the Available Fields list and inserts that field in the Selected Fields list. Repeat this step for each field that you want to include. (To add all the fields at once, click the >> button.) The figure shows the three fields that I selected to include in the report:

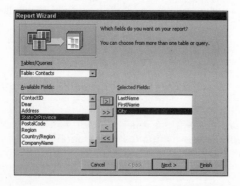

3. After you select all the fields that you want to include, click the Next button. The Report Wizard dialog box asks its next question, as shown in the figure:

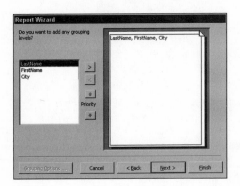

4. If you want to group the records together based on a field, select the field that you want to use for the grouping in the list on the left side of the dialog box, then click >.

5. Click the Next button. The wizard asks about the sort order for the grouped items in the report, as shown in the figure.

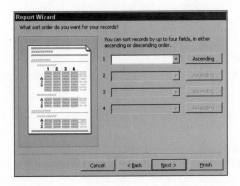

6. Use the first drop-down list to select the first field by which you want to sort the report. You can sort the report by up to four fields, and each field can be used to sort the report in Ascending or Descending sequence.

7. Click the Next button. The wizard asks how you want the report formatted, as shown in this dialog box:

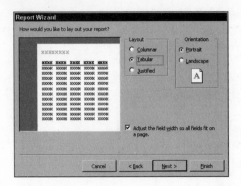

8. You can select the organization of the report on the page —
choosing whether it appears as Portrait or Landscape orienta-
tion, and whether you want the field widths adjusted automatically so that all fit on the page. When you have determined the
layout for your report, click the Next button. The wizard then
asks you what style to use for the report, as shown in the figure:

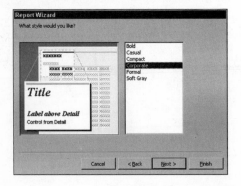

9. From the list, select the report style that suits your fancy and
then click the Next button. The Report Wizard dialog box asks
its final question, as shown in the figure:

10. Change the report title in the text box if you don't like the one that the wizard proposes, and then click the Finish button. The wizard grinds and churns for a few moments while creating the report, and then the wizard displays the report in Preview mode, as shown in the figure:

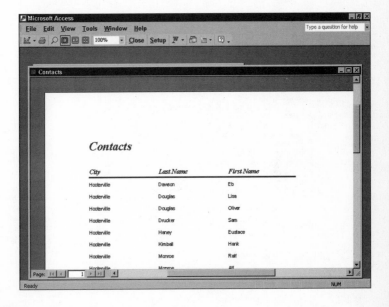

11. To print the report, click the Print button on the Standard toolbar.

12. To save your report design, choose File⇨Save.

Outlook 2002

This part covers Outlook, the all-in-one personal information manager that comes with Microsoft Office XP. Outlook functions as an address book, a calendar, and a task organizer, and it can even double as your e-mail program. For more information about Outlook, pick up a copy of *Microsoft Outlook 2002 For Dummies,* by Bill Dyszel, published by Hungry Minds, Inc.

In this part . . .

Calendar

One of Outlook's primary functions is keeping a calendar so that you can track appointments and upcoming events. To switch to the Outlook calendar, click the Calendar icon in the Outlook Bar (the Outlook Bar is the list of icons along the left edge of the Outlook window) or choose Go⇨Calendar. The figure shows what Outlook's calendar looks like:

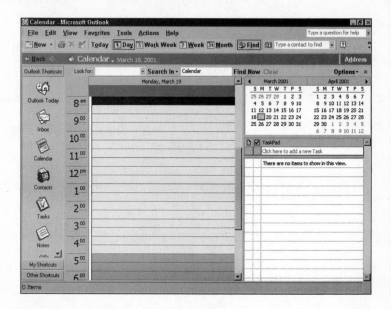

The following sections describe the most common procedures for using the Outlook calendar.

Views

Outlook gives you four different views for working with your calendar: Day, Work Week, Week, and Month. To change views, click the following buttons in the toolbar:

    ✔ Day

    ✔ Work Week

    ✔ Week

    ✔ Month

The calendar also lets you view active appointments, scheduled lists, annual events, and recurring appointments. You can see these views by choosing the View⇨Current View command.

If you don't like the plain vanilla calendar view, you can use the commands on the View⇨Current View menu to switch among several alternate ways to view your calendar. For example, View⇨Current View⇨Events displays your calendar as a list of events, and View⇨ Current View⇨Active Appointments lets you focus on your appointments. You can also use the View⇨Current View⇨Customize command to customize your calendar view.

Scheduling an appointment

To schedule an appointment, follow these steps:

1. Switch to the calendar view in which you prefer to work. Daily or weekly views are best for scheduling appointments. *See also* "Views."

2. Click the day on which you want to schedule the appointment.

3. Click the time slot during which you want to schedule the appointment. If you want the appointment to stretch beyond a single time interval, drag the mouse across the desired time periods.

4. Type a description for the appointment. With that, you're done. The figure shows a scheduled lunch appointment, shown in Day view:

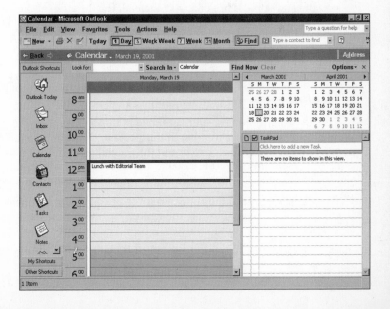

Canceling an appointment

To cancel an appointment, follow these steps:

1. In the calendar, highlight the appointment that you want to cancel.

2. Click the Delete button. The appointment disappears from the calendar.

Rescheduling an appointment

Here's the procedure for rescheduling an appointment by dragging it to a new time or date:

1. Switch to a calendar view that shows both the appointment that you want to reschedule and the date to which you want to reschedule it. To move an appointment to a different time on the same day, for example, switch to Day view. To reschedule to a different day in the same week, switch to Week view. *See also* "Views."

2. Click the appointment to select it.

3. Drag the appointment to the new time and/or day.

You can also reschedule an appointment by double-clicking the appointment. This opens the Appointment dialog box, in which you can adjust the Start Time and End Time fields in the dialog box. (If you change the start time, the end time is automatically adjusted to keep the appointment the same length. If you change the end time, the start time is not changed. Instead, the duration of the appointment changes.)

Recurring appointments

You can use Outlook to schedule recurring appointments, such as staff meetings or other annoying appointments that you hate to go to every day, week, or month. Here's the procedure:

1. Follow the procedure outlined in the section "Scheduling an appointment" (earlier in this part) to create an appointment for the next occurrence of the recurring date. If you have a staff meeting from 12:00 to 1:30 every Friday afternoon, for example, schedule the appointment for next Friday.

2. Double-click the appointment to open the Appointment window, as shown in the figure:

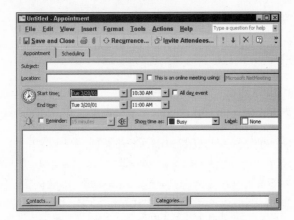

3. Click the Recurrence button to open the Appointment Recurrence dialog box, as shown in the figure:

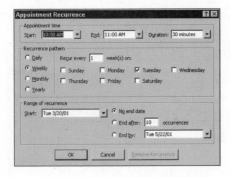

Outlook initially assumes that the appointment occurs every week on the same day and time. If this is not the case (for example, if the appointment should be every other week or once a month), you can make changes by following the next step.

4. If necessary, change the Recurrence Pattern options to indicate the frequency of the appointment (Daily, Weekly, Monthly, or Yearly). If you change the frequency option, a new set of controls appears in the Recurrence Pattern area of the Appointment Recurrence dialog box, enabling you to specify the exact schedule for the recurring appointment. To schedule an appointment that occurs only on the fourth Friday of every month, for example, click Monthly. A set of list box controls appears, enabling you to specify that the appointment occurs on a certain day each month — in this case, on the fourth Friday.

5. Click OK and then click the Save and Close button.

Outlook adds a special icon to the appointment in the calendar to indicate that the appointment is recurring.

Events

An *event* is an item that occurs on a specific calendar date but does not have a particular time associated with it. Examples of events include birthdays, anniversaries, vacations, and so on.

To add an event to your calendar, follow these steps:

1. Switch to the calendar view in which you want to work — Day, Week, or Month. *See also* "Views."

2. In the calendar, click the date on which the event occurs.

3. Select Actions⇨New All Day Event from the menu bar. The Event dialog box appears, as shown in the figure:

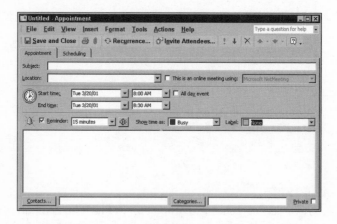

4. Type a description for the event in the Subject box.

5. If the event continues for more than one day, change the end date by selecting a date from the End Time drop-down list.

6. If it is a reminder of a birthday, anniversary, or some other similar event, make sure that the All Day Event check box is checked.

7. The Show Time As drop-down list allows you to set to the Free option, which reminds you of the date but doesn't block your day from other appointments.

8. If this is a personal matter, make sure that the Private check box is marked. This prevents other people on your network from receiving this message.

9. After all the features are marked, click the Save and Close button. The event appears on your calendar.

The figure shows how a typical event appears in Daily Calendar view:

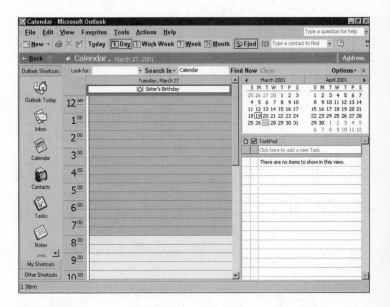

Meetings

If everyone in your office uses Outlook and your computers are connected by a network, you can use the Plan a Meeting feature to schedule office meetings electronically. Outlook automatically picks a time slot that's available for each participant and notifies each person of the time and place of the meeting.

Follow these steps to plan a meeting:

1. Choose Actions⇨Plan a Meeting. The Plan a Meeting dialog box appears, as shown in the figure:

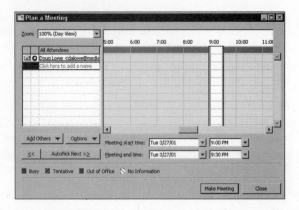

2. Type the names of the people who need to attend the meeting in the All Attendees column. Or click the Add Others button, and then choose Add From Address Book to call up a dialog box that lets you select names from your address book. After you select everyone that you want to invite, click OK to return to the Plan a Meeting dialog box. Outlook reviews each person's schedule so that you can see who has free time (and when).

3. Pick a time when everyone is free by clicking the time in the schedule area of the Appointment dialog box. Or click AutoPick to allow Outlook to pick the time for you.

4. Click the Make Meeting button. Outlook displays the following window:

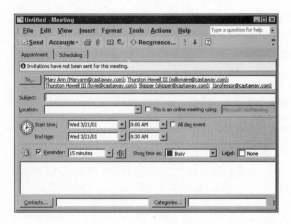

5. Type a subject for the meeting invitation in the Subject box and a location in the Location box.

6. Click the Send button to send the invitations.

If someone invites you to a meeting, you receive an e-mail message that includes three buttons that you can click to reply to the invitation: Accept, Decline, or Tentative. Click the appropriate button to reply to the invitation.

Contacts

Outlook keeps an address book, which it refers to as *contacts*. To work with contacts, click the Contacts icon in the Outlook Shortcuts list on the left edge of the Outlook window, or choose View⇨Go To⇨Contacts. Here's how Outlook appears when you call up your contacts:

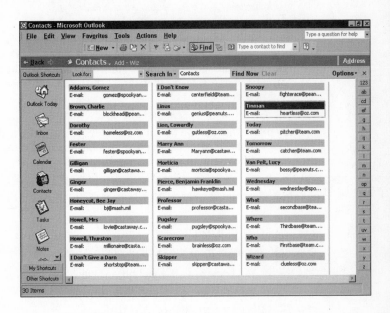

You can use the following procedures to maintain your contacts.

Adding a contact

To add a new contact to Outlook, follow these steps:

  1. Click the New Contact button in the toolbar or choose File⇨New⇨Contact from the menu. (Or, if you like keyboard shortcuts, press Ctrl+N.) The following dialog box appears:

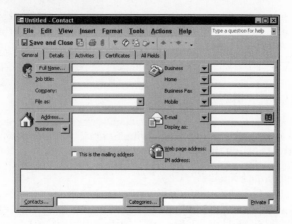

2. In the Personal tab of the dialog box fill in the contact's name, telephone numbers, addresses, and e-mail address. The bottom of the box has a window that shows the e-mail addresses of your new contact.

3. The other tabs in this dialog box allow you to make notes regarding this person for future reference, and give you the opportunity to enter a great deal of information that may or may not be useful to you.

 4. When you've added all the desired information for your contact, click the Save and Close button.

Deleting a contact

To delete a contact from the Outlook contact list, follow these steps:

1. Switch to Contacts view by choosing View⇨Go To⇨Contacts or by clicking the Contacts icon in the Outlook Shortcuts list.

2. Click the contact that you want to delete.

3. Click the Delete button.

If you realize that deleting your best friend was a mistake, you can undo your rude action by choose Edit⇨Undo or pressing Ctrl+Z.

Updating a contact

If the address information (or any other information) for a contact changes, you can update the contact by following these steps:

1. Switch to Contacts view by choosing View⇨Go To⇨Contacts or by clicking the Contacts icon in the Outlook Shortcuts list.

2. Double-click the contact that you want to change to call up the dialog box containing information for the contact.

3. Enter any changes that you want to make in the various tabs of the Contact dialog box.

4. Click the Save and Close button. The Contact dialog box closes and your changes are automatically saved.

Distribution lists

A *distribution list* is a group of Address Book contacts. When you send an e-mail message to a distribution list, Outlook automatically sends a copy of the message to each person in the list.

To create a distribution list, follow these steps:

1. Click the down-arrow at the right of the New Contact button and choose Distribution List from the menu that appears. Or, if you prefer, choose File⇨New⇨Distribution List from the menu. The Distribution List dialog box appears, as shown in the figure:

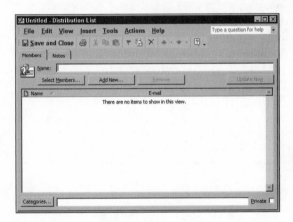

2. Click the Select Members button to call up the Select Members dialog box, shown in the figure:

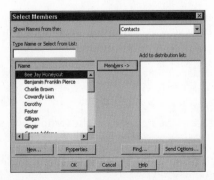

3. In the list box on the left side of the Select Members dialog box, click the name of a contact that you want to add to the distribution list. Then, click the Members-> button. Or, just double-click the contact's name. Either way, the contact is added to the list box on the right side of the Select Members dialog box.

4. Repeat Step 4 for each contact that you want to add to the distribution list.

5. After you're finished adding people to the distribution list, click OK. You're returned to the Distribution List dialog box. The names of the people that you added are now listed, as shown in the figure:

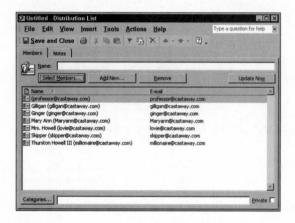

6. Type a name for the distribution list in the Name text box.

 7. Click Save and Close to save the list.

E-Mail

Outlook includes an integrated e-mail feature that can send and receive messages from your various e-mail services. If you receive e-mail from your local area network, from the Internet, or from the Microsoft Network, Outlook can read e-mail from all three sources. That way, you don't need to fuss around with three separate e-mail programs.

To access the Outlook e-mail feature, click the Inbox icon in the Outlook Shortcuts list at the right side of the Outlook window. The figure shows the inbox:

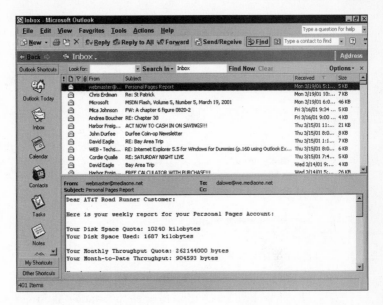

The following sections describe how to accomplish the most important tasks in using Outlook e-mail.

Reading e-mail

Reading e-mail is easy in Outlook. All you do is double-click the message that you want to read in the inbox. The message appears in its own window, as shown in the figure:

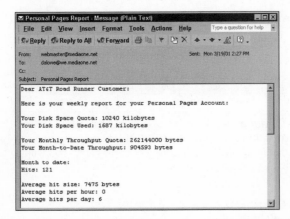

After you finish reading the message, close the window by clicking the Close button (the button with the X in the upper-right corner of the window). Or click any of the buttons described in the following list to respond to the message or to read other messages:

 ✔ Display the previous message in your inbox.

 ✔ Display the next message in your inbox.

 ✔ Reply to the sender.

 ✔ Reply to the sender and all other recipients of the original message.

 ✔ Forward the message to another user.

 ✔ Delete the message.

Replying to e-mail

To reply to an e-mail message, follow these steps:

 1. Click the Reply button to open the window shown in the figure:

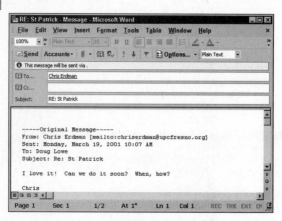

2. Type your response. Outlook automatically displays the contents of the original message below your response. You can delete as much of the original message as you want by selecting the text and pressing the Delete key.

 3. Click the Send button.

Sending e-mail

To send a new e-mail message, follow these steps:

 1. Click the New Mail button to make the dialog box shown in the figure appear:

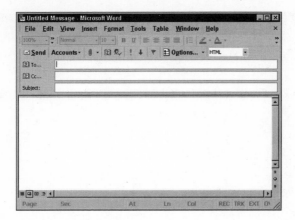

2. In the To text box, type the e-mail address of the recipient (or recipients). If you want to pick names from your Address Book, click the To button. A dialog box listing all your contacts with e-mail addresses appears; select the recipient that you want and then click OK.

3. Type the e-mail address of anyone that you want to receive a carbon copy of the message in the Cc field. To pick names from your Address Book, click the Cc button.

   You can also use the Bcc field to send a blind carbon copy. The main To recipient and the Cc recipients won't know about the Bcc recipients. To include Bcc recipients, click the Cc button to summon the Select Names dialog box, then use the Bcc-> button to add Bcc names.

4. Type the subject of your message in the Subject text box.

5. Type the body of your message in the message area — the large text box at the bottom of the Message dialog box.

6. Click the Send button in the toolbar.

To attach a file to your message, click the Insert File button to bring up an Insert File dialog box (which, unsurprisingly, looks just like the Open dialog box). Select the file that you want to attach from this dialog box and then click OK.

Tasks

Outlook enables you to keep a task list, which is a constant reminder that you have miles to go before you sleep . . . and miles to go before you sleep. The figure shows the Outlook task list:

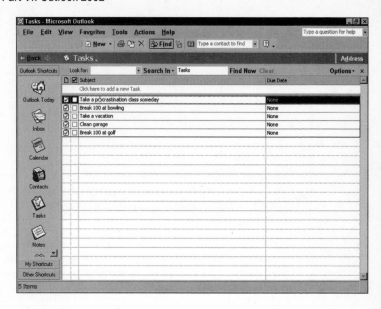

Creating a task

To add an item to your task list, switch to Tasks View by clicking the Tasks icon in the Outlook bar (shown in the margin). Then, follow these steps:

1. Click the New button. The New Task dialog box opens, as shown in the figure.

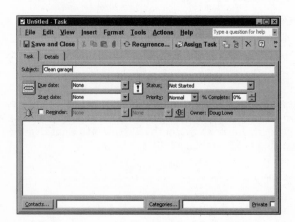

2. Fill in the New Task dialog box with the details of the task that you want to complete. The New Task dialog box has two tabs.

The Task tab allows you to fill in the general information about the task; this is what appears on the Task List. The Details tab allows you to keep a record of the work you do on the task. This tab is helpful for billing companies for your work.

3. After you have the task entered, click the Save and Close button. The task is then added to the top of the Task List.

Sigh. You have so much to do.

Task requests

Outlook allows you to create a task and then give it to someone else on your network. This is useful for distributing job assignments to subordinates or team members. One thing to always keep in mind is that as soon as you assign a task to another person — as far as Outlook is concerned — you give up ownership of the task. You can keep it in your Task List and receive updates from the person performing the task, but you can't change any of the information regarding the task. Only the person doing the work can do that.

To use Outlook to assign a task to another person:

1. Open the Task List by clicking the Task button on the left side of the Outlook window.

2. Click the arrow next to the New button on the toolbar to open the New Task drop-down list. Select Task Request from this list. The Task Request dialog box opens, as shown here:

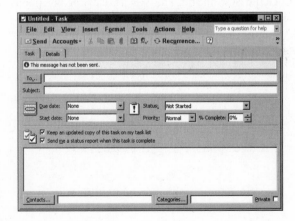

Notice that this looks like a cross between the New Task dialog box and the Send E-mail dialog box.

3. Enter the e-mail address of the person that you're assigning the job to in the To text box, or click the To button to see your address book. Enter the assignment in the Subject window and then complete the Due date and Start date list boxes. Use the other controls to indicate the Status of the task, its priority, and the percentage the task is already complete.

4. Put a check in the Keep an Updated Copy of This Task on My Task List check box if you want to track the other person's progress on this assignment. If you want to know when the task is finished, put a check in the Send Me a Status Report When This Task Is Complete check box.

5. Use the text box at the bottom of the Task Request to compose a message that politely asks the recipient of your task request to complete the task.

6. Click the Details tab and add any additional information you think might be helpful.

7. Click the Send button. The task request is sent.

The person who receives your task request can either accept or reject the task. Either way, Outlook automatically notifies you of the recipient's response.

Working with the Drawing Toolbar

The Arts and Crafts Division at Microsoft decided to endow as many Microsoft Office programs as possible with a Drawing toolbar, which enables you to doodle on your documents. The Drawing toolbar works the same way in Word, Excel, PowerPoint, FrontPage, and Publisher, so after you learn how to draw in one Office program, you can draw in all of them. If the Drawing toolbar is not visible, you can summon it by choosing View⇨Toolbars⇨Drawing.

In this part . . .

3-D Style

You can turn any shape into a three-dimensional object by using the 3-D Style button. To apply a 3-D effect to an object, first click the object to select it, then click the 3-D Style button. Then choose the 3-D effect that you want to use from the menu that appears as shown in the figure.

After you have applied a 3-D effect to an object, you can tweak the 3-D appearance by selecting the object, then clicking the 3-D Style button and choosing 3-D Settings from the menu that appears. This summons the 3-D Settings toolbar, as shown in the figure:

The following table describes the function of each button on the 3-D Settings toolbar:

Button	What it does
	Shows or hides the 3-D effect.
	Rotates the object down along its horizontal axis.
	Rotates the object up along its horizontal axis.
	Rotates the object right along its vertical axis.
	Rotates the object left along its vertical axis.
	Controls the depth of the 3-D surfaces.
	Controls the direction of the 3-D surfaces.

Button	What it does
	Controls the placement of the light source for the 3-D effect.
	Selects one of four surface styles: Wireframe, Matte, Plastic, and Metal.
	Sets the color of the 3-D surfaces.

To change a three-dimensional object back to two dimensions, click the 3-D Style button and choose No 3-D from the menu that appears.

 Use the WordArt feature to create 3-D text effects. *See also* "WordArt."

Aligning and Distributing Objects

After you have created two or more drawing objects on your document, you can use the Draw⇨Align or Distribute command to line the objects up or space them out evenly.

 Another way to align or distribute objects is to use the Grid, which helps you visually line up objects as you draw them by displaying a neat array of little dots on the drawing area. *See also* "Grid."

To line up or space out two or more objects, follow these steps:

1. Select the objects that you want to line up or space out by clicking one of the objects, and then holding down Shift while clicking the other objects.

2. Click Draw⇨Align and Distribute.

3. Choose the type of alignment that you want to apply. You can choose from three types of horizontal alignment (left, center, and right), three types of vertical alignment (top, middle, and bottom), and two types of distribution (horizontal and vertical).

 If you want to center two or more objects directly over each other, align them twice: First use Align Center, and then use Align Middle.

 The order in which you select objects before you align them doesn't affect the way they are aligned or distributed. Instead, the objects are aligned relative to one another. For example, if you use Align Left, all of the objects that you selected are aligned with the leftmost object. And if you use Align Center, the selected objects are aligned with the center of the entire group of objects.

Arrows

 You can draw arrows several different ways in Microsoft Office. The easiest way is to use the Arrow button, shown in the margin. Just click the Arrow button, click in your document where you want the arrow to start, draw the mouse to where you want the arrow to end, and release the mouse button.

 You can change the shape of an arrowhead or you can add arrowheads to any line that you've previously drawn by clicking the Arrow Style button (shown in the margin). This brings up the Arrow Style menu, shown in the figure:

You can choose any of the arrow styles in the menu, or you can choose More Arrows to bring up the Format Autoshape dialog box:

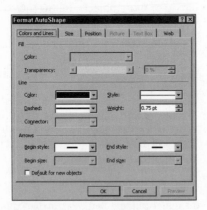

The controls at the bottom of this dialog box let you add arrowheads to the beginning or end of the line. The Begin Style and End Style drop-downs reveal the types of arrowheads that you can add:

You can also use the Begin Size and End Size drop-downs to select the size of the arrowheads. Click OK when you have adjusted the arrows to your liking.

You can also create arrows using AutoShapes. *See also* "AutoShapes."

AutoShapes

AutoShapes are a convenient way to draw commonly used shapes, such as rectangles, ovals, triangles, pentagons, stars, block arrows, and more. In all, more than 150 AutoShapes are at your disposal. When you click the AutoShapes button, a menu appears that organizes the AutoShapes into the following categories:

- ✔ **Lines:** Straight lines, curved lines, lines with arrowheads, scribbly lines, and a freeform tool that you can use to draw any imaginable shape.

- ✔ **Connectors:** Special lines that attach themselves to other objects and stay connected even when you move the objects.

- ✔ **Basic Shapes:** Basic geometric shapes, such as rectangles, parallelograms, ovals, and triangles — plus odd shapes, such as smiley faces, lightning bolts, and hearts.

- ✔ **Block Arrows:** Fat arrows pointing in various directions.

- ✔ **Flowchart:** Flowchart symbols.

- ✔ **Stars and Banners:** Multi-pointed stars and banner shapes that you can add text to.

- ✔ **Callouts:** Text boxes and speech bubbles like those used in comic strips.

- ✔ **More AutoShapes:** Almost 75 additional AutoShapes that don't fit neatly into the other categories, including other goodies, such as office furniture, a Christmas tree, and interlocking puzzle pieces.

Note that four of the most commonly used AutoShapes — Line, Arrow, Rectangle, and Oval — can be accessed directly on the Drawing toolbar. This saves you time and the trouble of contending with the AutoShapes menu when drawing these common shapes.

Drawing an AutoShape

To draw an AutoShape, follow these steps:

1. Click the AutoShapes button in the Drawing toolbar to summon the AutoShapes menu.

2. Choose the AutoShape category that you want. A toolbar appears displaying the choices for the category. The figure shows the Basic Shapes toolbar:

3. Click the AutoShape that you want to draw.

4. Click where you want the shape to appear, and then hold the mouse button and drag the shape to the desired size. When you release the mouse button, the shape appears and adopts the current fill color and line style.

Hold down Shift while you draw the shape if you want the shape to be undistorted — if you want to create a perfect circle or square, for example.

5. To add text, right-click the shape and choose Add Text from the menu that appears. Then type whatever text you want to appear in the shape. (Any AutoShape except for simple lines can contain text.)

6. If the AutoShape has one or more yellow drag diamonds, drag the diamonds to modify the shape. For example, the figure shows how you can change the shape of a cube, an arrow, and a banner by dragging the yellow diamonds in different ways:

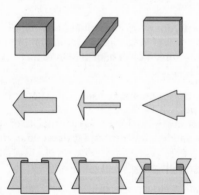

Drawing a freeform shape

One of the most useful AutoShapes is the Freeform shape, which is found in the Lines category of the AutoShapes menu. You can use the Freeform shape to draw a polygon or irregular shape with any number of straight or curved sides and in any shape you want. Here are some examples of shapes that you can draw with the Freeform tool:

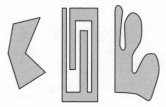

Here are the steps:

1. Click the AutoShape button and then choose <u>L</u>ines.

2. Click the Freeform button (shown in the margin).

3. Click where you want to position the first corner of the object.

4. Click where you want to position the second corner of the object in order to draw the first side of the shape.

5. To draw a curved side, hold down the mouse button and drag the mouse like a pencil to draw the side. Release the button when the side is finished.

6. Keep clicking to add straight sides or keep dragging to add curved sides.

7. To finish the shape, click near the first corner of the object (the one that you created in Step 3). The final side is added and the shape becomes a closed polygon.

Clip Art

Office comes with a large collection of clip art that you can place in any of your documents. Besides the clip art that comes on the Office CD, you can also get clip art from Microsoft's Clips Online Web site. All of this clip art is available to you simply by clicking the Insert Clip Art button.

Follow these steps to insert a Clip Art picture into your document:

1. Click the Insert Clip Art button. The Insert Clip Art pane appears, as shown in the figure. (Although the figure shows a Word document, the Insert Clip Art pane works the same in Excel, PowerPoint, Publisher, and FrontPage.)

Note that the first time you activate the Clip Gallery, you may get a dialog box offering to add your existing clip art to the Clip Gallery. Why not accept the invitation?

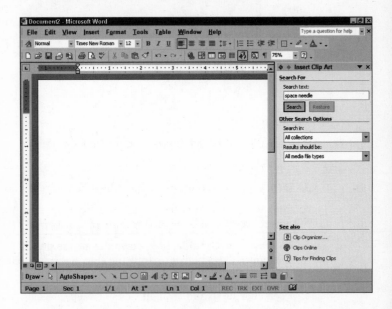

2. Type a word or phrase describing the picture that you want to find in the Search Text box.

3. Click the Search button. Pictures that meet your description appear in the Insert Clip Art pane. For example, I obtained the following results after searching for "Christmas:"

4. Click the picture that you want to use. The picture is inserted, as shown in the figure.

The clip art is probably too large or too small, so you can resize it by dragging one of the handles around the edge of the clip art.

You can click the Clip Organizer link near the bottom of the Insert Clip Art pane to call up the Clip Organizer, a stand-alone program that lets you organize and search for clip art. The figure shows the Clip Organizer program:

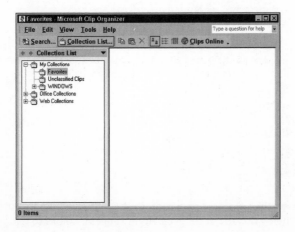

With the Media Gallery, you can search through the Office Clip Art collection by category, you can access Microsoft's Media Gallery Online collection, and you can organize your own collections of clip art pictures.

Colors and Fill Effects

The three color icons on the Drawing toolbar enable you to set the color for three types of objects:

- 🗸 **Fill Color:** Sets the interior color for closed shapes, such as rectangles, ovals, and so on.

- 🗸 **Font Color:** Sets the color for text fonts.

- 🗸 **Line Color:** Sets the color for lines.

Note that some objects have all three types of color. For example, a text box has a font color for the text within the box, a fill color for the box itself, and a line color for the line that encloses the box.

To set the fill, line, or font color for an object, first select the object, and then use the appropriate Color button. If you simply click the button, the object assumes the color that is currently shown in the button itself. If you want to apply a different color, click the arrow next to the button instead of the button itself to reveal a menu of colors. Then choose the color that you want to use from the menu.

If the color that you want doesn't appear in the Color menu, choose the More Colors command at the bottom of the menu. The following dialog box appears:

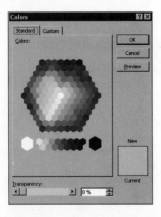

Choose the color that you want, or click the Custom tab at the top of the dialog box to see an even larger range of colors to choose from.

Use the Transparency slider near the bottom of the Colors dialog box to make the color transparent, allowing objects behind the object that you are coloring to show through.

 You can create fancy fill effects by choosing Fill Effects from the menu that appears when you click the Fill Color button. This action summons the following dialog box:

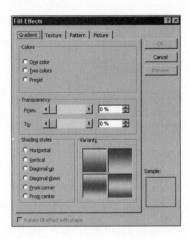

The tabs at the top of the Fill Effects dialog box let fill the object with a gradient (in which two colors are blended), a texture (such as marble or tissue paper), a pattern (such as diagonal lines or bricks), or a picture.

Diagrams

 Office includes a new feature called the Diagram Gallery that lets you easily create common types of diagrams. With the Diagram Gallery, you can create the following types of diagrams:

 ✔ **Cycle Diagram:** Shows a process with a continuous cycle.

 ✔ **Radial Diagram:** Shows relationships to a central core idea or element.

 ✔ **Pyramid Diagram:** Shows foundation-based relationships.

 ✔ **Venn Diagram:** Shows overlapping relationships.

✔ **Target Diagram:** Shows steps towards a goal.

The Diagram Gallery also allows you to create an organization chart. *See also* "Organization Chart."

To create a diagram, follow these steps:

1. Click the Insert Diagram button in the Drawing toolbar (shown in the margin). The Diagram Gallery dialog box appears, as shown in the figure:

2. Click the type of diagram that you want to create.

3. Click OK. The diagram is inserted into your document. The figure shows how a Cycle Diagram appears in a Word document:

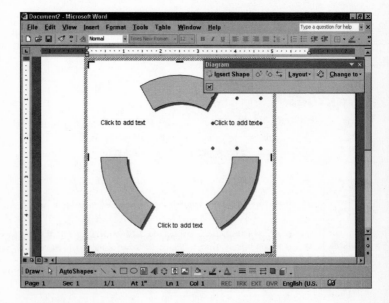

4. If necessary, resize the diagram by dragging any of the handles on the edge of the diagram.

5. Type text in each of the text boxes (labeled "Click to add text").

6. Each diagram is initially set up with three elements. To add another element, click the Insert Shape button in the Diagram toolbar. Each time you add an element, the other elements are adjusted to make room for the new shape.

To delete an element, click the element and press Delete. The other elements adjust to balance to diagram.

Other buttons on the Diagram toolbar allow you to change the order of elements in the diagram, change the diagram to a different type, and apply an autoformat to the diagram.

Grid

The Grid is a drawing aid that simplifies the task of lining up items when you are drawing. To change the grid settings, click Draw in the Drawing toolbar, then choose the Grid command. The dialog box shown in the figure appears:

If you check the Snap Objects to Grid checkbox, any objects that you draw in your document are automatically lined up at the nearest gridline. The other settings in the Drawing Grid dialog box let you set the spacing of grid lines and control whether the grid should be visible in your document while you are working.

The grid is never printed when you print your document, so you don't have to turn the grid off before you print.

Grouping

Grouping lets you combine drawing objects into a single object, which you can treat as a unit. Grouping is useful when you are working with complicated pictures involving many objects.

To create a group, select the objects that you want to group together, then click Draw in the Drawing toolbar and choose the Group command.

To take a group apart so that its individual elements become separate objects again, select the group, click Draw, and then choose the Ungroup command.

If you want to recreate a group after you've ungrouped it, you can do so by selecting any one object that was a part of the group, clicking Draw, and then choosing the Regroup command.

Line Styles

Three buttons on the Drawing toolbar let you change the style of lines in your drawings:

 ✓ **Line Style:** Sets the thickness of the lines that outline the object.

 ✓ **Dash Style:** Creates dashed lines.

✓ **Arrow Style:** Adds arrows to either end of the line.

To change a line style, first select the line that you want to change, click the appropriate button to call up a menu of options, and then choose the option that you want to apply.

For more precise control over the line style, click the Line Style button and choose More Lines from the menu that appears. This summons a dialog box that lets you set the line width, color, dash pattern, and arrowheads.

 For more information about the Arrow Style button, see the Arrows section earlier in this part.

Ordering Objects

When you draw more than one object, Office layers the objects on top of each other in the order in which you draw them. If two objects overlap, the one higher up on the drawing stack covers up the portion of the lower object that it overlaps.

You can change the order of the objects relative to one another by using one of four commands located on the Draw menu in the Drawing toolbar:

- ✔ **Draw⇨Order⇨Bring to Front:** Brings the selected object to the top of the drawing stack.

- ✔ **Draw⇨Order⇨Send to Back:** Sends the selected object to the bottom of the drawing stack.

- ✔ **Draw⇨Order⇨Bring Forward:** Brings the selected object one step closer to the top of the drawing stack.

- ✔ **Draw⇨Order⇨Send Backward:** Sends the selected object one step closer to the bottom of the drawing stack.

- ✔ **Draw⇨Order⇨Bring in Front of Text:** Places drawing objects on top of text.

- ✔ **Draw⇨Order⇨Send Behind Text:** Sends drawing objects behind text.

 To bring one object to the top of another, you sometimes have to use the Bring Forward command several times, because even though the objects appear adjacent to one another, other drawing objects may occupy the layers between them.

Organization Charts

 An Organization Chart is a type of diagram that shows hierarchical relationships. Previous versions of Office included a program called Microsoft Organization Chart for creating organization charts. With Office XP, Microsoft has replaced the Microsoft Organization Chart program with on option on the Diagram Gallery that simplifies the task of creating organization charts. *See also* "Diagrams."

To create an organization chart, follow these steps:

 1. Click the Insert Diagram button (shown in the margin) to summon the Diagram Gallery dialog box, as shown in the figure:

2. Click the Organization Chart icon, then click OK. A skeleton organization chart is inserted into your document, as shown in the figure:

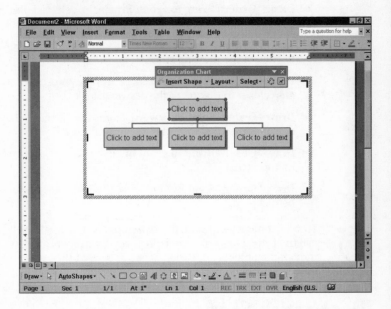

3. Click each box in the organization chart and type a name or any other text that you want to appear in the box.

4. To add a new box to the chart, first select an existing box in the organization chart. Then, click the down arrow next to the Insert Shape button in the Organization Chart toolbar and choose one of the following commands from the menu that appears:

   • **Subordinate:** Creates a new box subordinate to the selected box.

   • **Coworker:** Creates a new box at the same level as the selected box.

   • **Assistant:** Creates a new assistant box for the selected box. An assistant box is placed between the selected box and the selected box's subordinates.

5. To delete a box, right-click the box that you want to delete and choose Delete from the menu that appears. Or just click the box to select it, then press the Delete key.

Pictures

You can insert a picture file into your document by following these steps:

1. Click the Insert Picture button (shown in the margin). The Insert Picture dialog box appears, as shown in the figure:

2. Select the picture file that you want to insert. (If the file isn't listed in the Insert Picture dialog box, use the Look In drop-down control to locate the folder that contains the file you want to insert.)

3. Click Insert. The picture is inserted into your document.

4. Adjust the size of the picture if necessary by dragging any of the handles on the picture border.

The Picture toolbar contains buttons for working with pictures. If the Picture toolbar doesn't automatically appear when you select a picture, right-click the picture and choose the Show Picture Toolbar command from the menu. The following table lists the function of each button on the Picture toolbar:

Button	*What it does*
	Lets you display pictures in color, black and white, grayscale, or washed out.
	Increases the picture contrast.

cont.

Button	What it does
	Decreases the picture contrast.
	Increases the picture brightness.
	Decreases the picture brightness.
	Lets you crop the picture. Click the Crop button, and then grab the corners or edges of the picture to the crop out portions that you don't want to see.
	Sets the line style for the border around the picture.
	Calls up a dialog box that lets you compress pictures to save hard drive space.
	Calls up a dialog box that lets you format the picture object.
	Lets you set one color of the picture to be transparent. Click the Transparency Button, and then click a portion of the picture that is the color that you want to make transparent.
	Restores the picture to its original condition, removing contrast and brightness changes, cropping, and rotations.

Rotating and Flipping Objects

To *rotate* an object means to turn it about its center. To *flip* an object means to create a mirror image of the object. Office lets you rotate in 90-degree increments or freely rotate the object to any angle you want, and lets you flip any object horizontally or vertically.

Unfortunately, rotating an object with text (such as a text box) does *not* rotate the text in Word or Excel. However, it is possible to rotate text that you create with WordArt. *See also* "WordArt."

To flip an object, simply choose the object that you want to flip, then click the Draw button to reveal the Draw menu, choose Rotate or Flip, and then choose Flip Horizontal or Flip Vertical.

To rotate an object 90 degrees, choose the object, then click the Draw button to reveal the Draw menu, choose Rotate or Flip, and then choose Rotate Left or Rotate Right.

To spin an object to any angle you want, click the object, then spin the object by dragging the green rotation handle. (If the object does not have a green rotation handle, the object cannot be rotated.)

To rotate an object in 15-degree increments, hold down Shift while you drag the green rotation handle.

Shadows

You can apply a shadow to any drawing object by selecting the object and clicking the Shadow button, shown in the margin. The Shadow menu appears, as shown in the figure:

Click the shadow style that you want to use.

If you click Shadow Settings, the Shadow Settings toolbar appears. This toolbar contains buttons that let you nudge the shadow into exactly the right position and change the shadow color to create a custom shadow effect.

Text Boxes

A text box allows you to put text anywhere you want on your document. To create a text box, click the Text Box tool in the Drawing toolbar (shown in the margin), and draw the shape of the text box on the document. Then, start typing. You can use the normal text formatting features of the program that you're working in to format the text within the text box.

You can remove the border that is normally drawn around a text box by selecting the text box, then clicking the Line Color button and choosing No Line from the menu that appears.

WordArt

Microsoft WordArt is specially designed for formatting text in strange ways. You usually use it to create logos. Although the name suggests that WordArt is intended to be used alongside Word, it works just as well with PowerPoint, Excel, Publisher, FrontPage, and even Access.

Follow these steps to create WordArt:

1. Click the Insert WordArt button (shown in the margin). The WordArt Gallery appears, as shown in the figure:

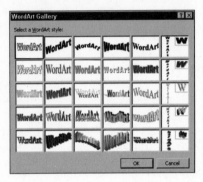

2. Pick the WordArt style you like, and then click OK. The Edit WordArt Text dialog box appears:

3. Type the text that you want to use and change the font.

4. Click OK. The WordArt object is created in your document, and the WordArt toolbar appears as shown in the figure:

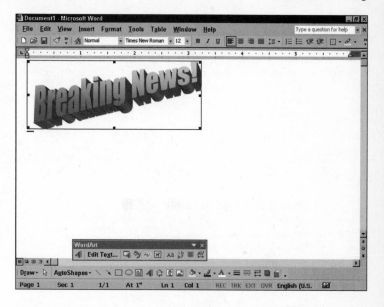

5. Fool around with the controls on the toolbar if you want. The function of each button is described in the following table:

Button	What it does
◢	Creates another WordArt object
🖉	Summons the Edit WordArt Text dialog box so you can change the text.
🖼	Summons the WordArt Gallery so you can quickly apply a different format.
A̶b̶c̶	Lets you change the shape of the WordArt text.
Aa	Alternates between normal letters and same height letters, in which upper and lower case letters are the same height.
A̶b̶ b̶	Alternates between horizontal and vertical text.
☰	Changes the alignment.
A̶V̶	Changes the space between letters.

6. Click anywhere outside the WordArt object frame to return to the program from which you called WordArt.

Part VIII

Completing Complex Tasks

Welcome to the advanced class! The tasks described in this part are features of Office XP that go beyond the skills of the average user. You can use them to impress your boss and make your co-workers jealous. The great thing about all these tasks is that they work in most or all the Office XP applications. Sure, some of them may look a little different in Word than they do in PowerPoint, and they may even work a little differently between the two programs, but once you get the hang of it, you'll know how to use any of these tools in any program that supports them.

In this part . . .

Embedding Objects in Your Documents

Embedding is the procedure where you take a section of one file in one application and make it a part of another. For example, you could take a chart from Excel, or a table from Access, or a graphic image, and embed it into a Word document. Or, you could take a body of text from Word and embed it into an Excel spreadsheet or into a PowerPoint slide.

Generally, you want to embed only objects that are files of limited size (smaller than a single page). If you want to have access to the information in a larger file, I suggest you use a hyperlink instead. See "Hyperlinks" later in this part for information on this very useful tool.

Creating a new embedded object

Office lets you create a new embedded object in your destination file and then enter the data or text that fits your needs. Basically, what you're doing is creating an area where a different application (the source application) determines the appearance and formatting of the destination file. For this set of steps, I embed an Excel chart into a Word document.

To create a new embedded object in a destination file:

1. Open the document in which you want to embed an object and position the cursor at the point where you want the new object to be inserted.

2. Select Insert⇨Object from the menu bar. The Object dialog box opens.

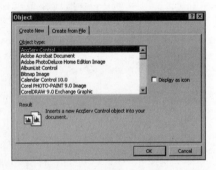

3. On the Create New tab, scroll down the Object type list until you find the application that you want to use for your embedded object (in this case, Microsoft Excel Chart). Highlight your selection and then click OK.

(Note that the object types that appear in the Object dialog box depend on the applications that are installed on your computer.)

4. The object is inserted into your document.

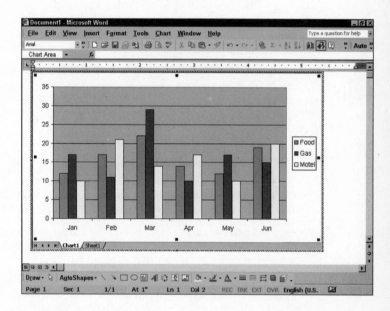

5. Edit the object using commands and toolbar buttons that apply to the object. For example, notice in the previous figure that a Chart menu is available. You can use the commands on the Chart menu to format the chart however you want. Also, the Sheet1 tab below the chart lets you switch to the datasheet the chart is based on so you can enter your own chart labels and data.

6. Click anywhere outside the embedded object to return to the document that contains the embedded object.

You can edit an embedded object at any time by double-clicking the object.

Embedding an object from an existing file

To insert an existing file as an embedded object, follow these steps:

1. In the program and file into which you want the existing file inserted, position the insertion point where you want the embedded object to appear.

2. Choose the Insert⇨Object command to summon the Object dialog box.

3. Click the Create from File tab. The dialog box appears as shown in the figure.

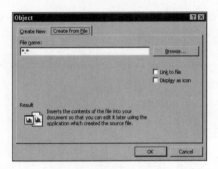

4. Click the Browse button. Doing so brings up a Browse dialog box, which is similar to the familiar Open dialog box.

5. Select the file you want to embed. If the file is not immediately visible in the Browse dialog box, use the Look In control to locate the drive and folder that contains the file.

6. Click OK to return to the Object dialog box and then click OK again. The file is inserted as an object.

Hyperlinks

Hyperlinks are "hot spots" in an Office document that, when clicked, jump to a specific location within the current document, open another Office document, or display a page from the World Wide Web. By creating hyperlinks to other Office documents, you can effectively share information among documents without going to the trouble of using OLE or the Paste Link command. For example, a Word document that contains a marketing proposal may include a hyperlink to an Excel spreadsheet that contains all the specific figures.

You can create a hyperlink in Word, Excel, PowerPoint, Access, FrontPage (but the process looks quite a bit different), or in the Web Page option of Publisher. To create a hyperlink, simply follow these steps:

1. Open the document in which you want to create a hyperlink.

2. Highlight the text or object that you want to be the hyperlink — that is, the text or the object that you want the user to click for the hyperlink.

3. Click the Insert Hyperlink button (shown in the margin), select Insert⇨Hyperlink, or press Ctrl+K. An Insert Hyperlink dialog box appears.

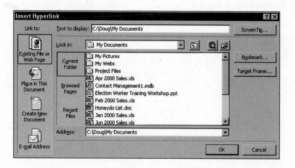

4. If you did not highlight something in the source document before opening the dialog box, click the top text box, Text to Display, and type in the text that becomes the hyperlink in your source document. To the right of this text box is the ScreenTip button. If you click it, you get another dialog box that allows you to type in text that then appears in a small floating window whenever a cursor is positioned over the displayed hyperlink text.

5. Along the left side of the Insert Hyperlink dialog box are four buttons that allow you to control where the hyperlink actually goes. Each button opens a different dialog box that allows you to determine the destination of the hyperlink. Click one of the four options, as described here:

- The Existing File or Web Page button (shown in the previous figure) helps you locate other files or Web pages to be opened with the hyperlink. This only works with other files that your computer can reach (because they are on your hard drive), can be reached over an intranet, or can be found on the World Wide Web. You can browse for a File, a Web Page, or a Bookmark or select from a list of Recent Files, Browsed Pages, or other Inserted Links. When you find the file you want to send your reader to, highlight it and click OK.

- The Place in This Document button sends the reader to another location in the same document to connect via the hyperlink. You may have to create a bookmark to get the hyperlink to go exactly where you want. Simply select the option that you want to send the reader to and click OK.

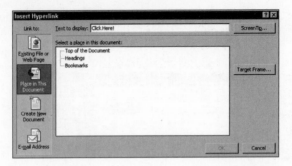

- The Create New Document button opens a new document window (of the same application you've been working with) that you can use to create a whole new destination document. Simply type in the filename for the new file, click Change to locate the directory where you want the destination file to go, and click OK. The new document opens before your eyes already linked to the source file.

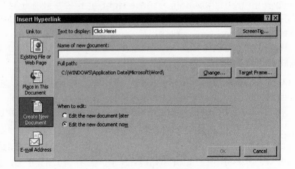

- The E-mail Address button opens a window that allows your reader to send e-mail to a particular e-mail address just by clicking the hyperlink. All you have to do is type in the e-mail address of the person you want the e-mail sent to, enter a subject line (though that is optional), and click OK. Whenever your reader clicks the hyperlink in the source document, Outlook opens a Send Mail window with the address already entered. Your readers can simply write whatever they want and click the Send button. Of course, this assumes that the reader uses Outlook Express for her e-mail. If she doesn't, then this hyperlink is of no use to her.

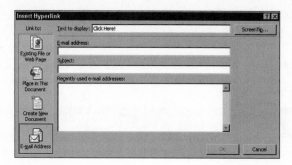

Links

Copying data from one program to another is easy enough, but what happens if you need to change the data? If you simply copy the data, you must track down every file to which you copied the data and update the data in each file. But if you link the data, any changes that you make to the original version of the data (the source file) automatically apply to copies of the linked data in the destination files.

Linking data

To copy data from one program to another and create a link, follow these steps:

1. Open the document that contains the data that you want to copy with the program you used to create the data. For example, if you want to copy spreadsheet data, open the spreadsheet with Excel.

2. Highlight the data that you want to copy by using the mouse or keyboard.

 3. Choose the Edit⇨Copy command or press Ctrl+C or click the Copy button, which appears on the Standard toolbar of all the Office programs.

4. Switch to the document and program into which you want to paste the data. For example, if you want to paste the data into a Word document, open the document with Word.

5. Position the insertion point where you want to insert the data.

6. Use the Edit⇨Paste command or click the Paste button (shown in the margin) or press Ctrl+V. The information from the other document is pasted into the document.

7. Click the Paste Options button that appears next to the pasted data to reveal the Paste Options menu, as shown in the figure.

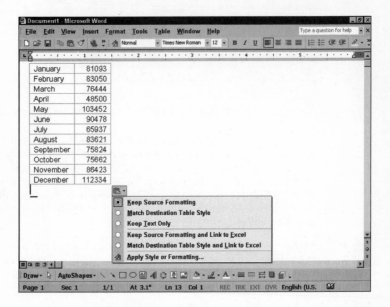

8. Choose the command that enables you to link to the program used to create the data. The exact wording of this command will vary. For the previous figure, either the "Keep Source Formatting and Link to Excel" command or "Match Destination Table Style and Link to Excel" command will do the trick.

Whenever you open the file that contains the link, the program checks to see whether the data has changed. If so, it updates the link.

Breaking a link

If you grow tired of the link and want to break it, follow this procedure:

1. Open the destination file for the link.

2. Choose Edit⇨Links. The Links dialog box appears.

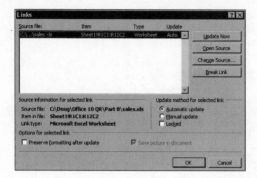

3. Select the link that you want to break from the Source file list.

4. Click the Break Link button.

5. When asked whether you really want to break the link, click the Yes button.

6. If other links still remain in the document, you need to click OK to dismiss the Links dialog box. If you break the last link, the Links dialog box automatically vanishes.

The fastest way to remove a link from a destination file is to click on the object to select it and press the Delete key. The linked file goes away.

Macros

Macros enable you to record the commands you need to carry out common procedures. If you find yourself performing the same sequence of operations over and over again, you can often save a lot of time by recording these actions in a macro. Then, whenever you need to perform that repetitive task, all you need to do is click a button, and the macro performs the task for you. The following procedures apply to Word, Excel, and PowerPoint.

Recording a macro

To record a macro, follow these steps:

1. Think about what you're going to do and rehearse the procedure to make sure that you really know what you're doing.

2. Choose Tools⇨Macro⇨Record New Macro to open the Record Macro dialog box.

This dialog box varies just slightly among Word, Excel, and PowerPoint. Here's how the Record Macro dialog box appears in Word:

3. Type the name of your macro in the Macro name text box.

4. To make your macro accessible from a toolbar or the keyboard, click either the Toolbars or Keyboard button, assign the shortcut, and then click the Close button. To help you assign the keyboard shortcut, a dialog box appears with a text box in which you can type the shortcut. Type the shortcut key that you want to use, click the Assign button, and then click the Close button.

   Note: The capability to assign the recorded macro to a keyboard shortcut while recording the macro is available only in Word. To assign a macro to a keyboard shortcut in PowerPoint or Excel, use the Tools⇨Customize command.

5. If you did not assign a keyboard shortcut in Step 4, click OK to begin recording the macro. A little macro recorder toolbox appears, as shown here:

6. Type the keystrokes and menu commands that you want to record in the macro. Click the Pause Recording button in the macro toolbox if you need to temporarily suspend recording; click the Pause Recording button again to resume recording.

7. After you finish recording, click the Stop Recording button.

You can now run the macro by using the procedure described in the following section, "Running a macro." If the macro doesn't work, you may have made a mistake while recording it. Record the macro again.

To delete a macro that you recorded incorrectly, choose Tools⇨ Macro⇨Macros to open the Macros dialog box. Select the macro you want to delete and then click the Delete button.

Running a macro

Follow this procedure to run a macro you previously recorded:

1. Choose Tools⇨Macro⇨Macros to access the Macro dialog box. (If you prefer keyboard shortcuts, press Alt+F8 instead.)

2. Select the macro you want to run from the list of macros currently available.

3. Click the Run button.

 If you assigned a keyboard shortcut or toolbar button to the macro, you can run the macro by pressing the assigned keyboard shortcut or clicking the macro's button.

Sharing Information Between Office Programs

This section describes several Office features that are specifically designed to allow you to exchange information between Word and Excel.

Exchanging tables between Word and Excel

When you copy or cut a range of cells from an Excel worksheet and paste it into Word, the worksheet data automatically converts to a Word table. If the Excel worksheet includes formulas, the formulas' calculated values are pasted into Word.

Likewise, when you copy or cut a Word table to the Clipboard and then paste it into Excel, the table data automatically converts to worksheet cells.

Inserting an Excel worksheet in a Word document

To insert an empty Excel worksheet object into a Word document, follow the procedure described under "Creating a new embedded object," earlier in this part. In the Object dialog box, specify Microsoft Excel Worksheet as the object type.

 You can also use the Insert Excel Worksheet button from the Standard toolbar.

Converting a PowerPoint presentation to Word

PowerPoint lets you convert a presentation to a Microsoft Word document by following these steps:

1. In PowerPoint, open the presentation that you want to convert.

2. Choose File⇨Send To⇨Microsoft Word. The Send to Microsoft Word dialog box appears, as shown in the figure:

3. The Send to Microsoft Word dialog box provides several options for how you want the presentation formatted in Word. Choose the formatting option you want.

4. Click OK, then wait while Send to Microsoft Word fires up Word and converts your presentation to a document.

5. When the presentation arrives in Word, choose File⇨Save if you want to save the file.

Converting a Word document to PowerPoint

You can convert a Word document to a PowerPoint presentation provided that the Word document uses standard heading styles to indicate its outline. Here's the procedure:

1. In Word, open the document you want to convert.

2. Choose the File⇨Send To⇨Microsoft PowerPoint command.

3. Word fires up PowerPoint and creates a presentation based on the headings in the document.

Another way to convert a Word document to a PowerPoint presentation is to open a new presentation in PowerPoint, then choose the Insert⇨Slides from Outline command and select the document you want to convert.

Using Access data in a mail merge

The Merge It With Word command provides an easy way to use Access data in a Word mail merge. Just follow these steps:

1. In Access, open the database that contains the table or query that you want to use in a mail merge.

2. In the main database window, click Table or Queries and select the table or query that you want to use.

3. Choose Tools⇨Office Links⇨Merge It with Microsoft Word. The Microsoft Word Mail Merge Wizard appears as shown in the figure:

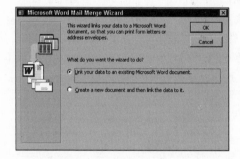

4. If the letter that you want to use for the mail merge already exists, click "Link your data to an existing Microsoft Word document," and then click the OK button. The Select Microsoft Word Document dialog box appears, which resembles a normal Open dialog box. Locate and select the Word document you want to use for your mailing. If you have not yet created the letter, choose Create a new document and then link the data to it. Then click OK.

5. Word starts up and activates the Mail Merge pane with the data source already set to the Access table or query you selected in Step 2. For the rest of the procedure, refer to "Mail Merging" in Part II of this book.

Converting Access data to a Word table

You can convert an Access table, query, form, or report to a Word table by using the Publish It With Microsoft Word command. Here is the procedure:

1. In Access, open the database that contains the database object that you want to convert to a Word document.

2. Select the database object (a table, query, form, or report) that you want to convert.

3. Choose Tools⇨Office Links⇨Publish It With Microsoft Word.

4. Watch as Access converts the data to a Word document.

Converting Access data to Excel

You can convert an Access table, query, form, or report to an Excel spreadsheet by using the Analyze It With Microsoft Excel command. Just follow these steps:

1. In Access, open the database that contains the database object that you want to convert to an Excel spreadsheet.

2. Select the database object (a table, query, form, or report) that you want to convert.

3. Choose Tools⇨Office Links⇨Analyze It With Microsoft Excel.

4. Watch as Access launches Excel and converts the data.

Index

FOR DUMMIES®

A world of resources to help you grow

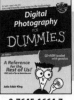

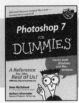

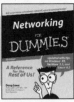